Wake Up and Live

Wake Up and Live

Dorothea Brande

DD BOOKS

Publishers for New Generations

This book is an Illustration, although the publisher has made every effort to Illustrate this book but there may still be some grammatical errors in it. If any such thing is found please contact us at the email below.
Every effort has been made to ensure the accuracy of this book's content. However, the publisher assumes no legal liability for errors or omissions. It is not the publisher's intention to offend any reader.

First Published: 2024

Book Name: Wake Up and Live (Illustrated)

Author: Dorothea Brande

Illustrated by **DD Books**

Price: 250/-

ISBN: 978-93-5957-401-1

Published by **DD BOOKS**

Email: **ddsalesglobal@gmail.com**

Table of Content

Introduction......7

1) Why Do We Fail?......13

2) The Will to Fail......19

3) Victims of the Will to Fail......26

4) The Rewards of Failure......34

5) Righting the Direction......45

6) The System in Operation......55

7) Warnings and Qualifications......65

8) On Saving Breath......70

9) The Task of the Imagination......77

10) On Codes and Standards......84

11) Twelve Disciplines......92

12) —And the Best of Luck!......112

Introduction

Two years ago, I stumbled upon a success formula that revolutionized my life. It was so simple and apparent that, once understood, I could hardly believe its role in the magical results that followed its implementation.

Firstly, I must confess that two years ago, I considered myself a failure. While others were oblivious to it, those who knew me well could see that I was only accomplishing a fraction of my potential. Despite holding an intriguing position and leading a moderately interesting life, deep down, I acknowledged my failure. What I engaged in was a mere substitute for what I had initially planned. No matter how cleverly I justified my lack of success with ingenious theories, I knew I should be doing more meaningful and genuine work.

Naturally, I was always seeking an escape from my predicament. However, when I fortuitously discovered the solution, I initially couldn't believe my luck. I refrained from dissecting or explaining it immediately. The formula's effects were so extraordinary that I almost started to attribute them to superstition; it felt like magic, and questioning the reasons behind a spell or incantation seemed unwise. Moreover, there was still a lingering wariness in my attitude at that time. I had attempted to overcome my challenges multiple times before, seemingly on the brink of success, only to find myself trapped again.

The primary reason for my reluctance to analyze or explain the formula's effects in detail was my busy schedule and the sheer enjoyment I derived from it. I reveled in the newfound ease with which I tackled tasks previously deemed impossible, witnessed barriers I thought were impenetrable dissolve, and felt the years-long inertia and timidity falling away like unlocked fetters.

I had been stuck in a deadlock for years, despite choosing my life's work, writing, early on and commencing with high hopes. Most of my completed work received a positive reception. However, when attempting to progress to a more mature phase, it felt as if I had been turned to stone, paralyzed and unable to move forward.

Certainly, it's undeniable that I was unhappy. Not miserably or agonizingly unhappy, but constantly bothered and disheartened by my own lack of effectiveness. Faced with a perceived failure in the more creative realms of literature, I immersed myself in editing. Relentlessly, I sought guidance from teachers, analysts, psychologists, and physicians, attempting to extricate myself from this pit. I read, inquired, thought, and worried, testing every suggested remedy. However, nothing offered more than temporary relief. While I could engage in feverish activity for a short period, it always ended abruptly, leaving me no closer to my goal and increasingly disheartened.

Then, in a moment between one minute and the next, I stumbled upon the idea that liberated me. Unintentionally, as I delved into research in another field, I encountered a sentence in the book "HUMAN PERSONALITY" by F. W. H. Myers that was so enlightening, I set the book aside to contemplate the myriad ideas inspired by that one profound hypothesis. When I resumed reading, I was a transformed person.

Every aspect, attitude, and relation of my life underwent a profound alteration. Initially, I wasn't aware of it; however, with growing certainty each day, I realized I had discovered a talisman to counteract failure, inertia, and discouragement, and it worked. That knowledge sufficed for me. My hands and days were so occupied that there was no time for introspection. Sometimes, as I drifted off to sleep after accomplishing in a short time what once felt like a colossal task, I'd think, like the old lady in the nursery rhyme, "This is none of I!" Yet, beyond doubt, "I" was reaping the rewards. The books I had longed to write, previously agonizingly elusive, flowed onto paper as swiftly as words could be penned. Far from feeling drained, I consistently discovered new ideas that had been concealed behind the mental barrier created by the backlog of work.

Here's the sum total of my writing output in the twenty years before discovering my formula—a meager amount achieved with great difficulty and protest. For safety's sake, I've exaggerated the items in each classification, resulting in a generous estimate: seventeen short stories, twenty book reviews, half a dozen newspaper items, and one abandoned attempt at a novel, completed less than a third of the way. An average of less than two finished pieces of work per year!

In the two years following my moment of enlightenment, here is the record: Three books (the first two within just two weeks less than the first year, both successful in their respective fields), twenty-four articles, four short stories, seventy-two lectures, the groundwork for three more books, and numerous letters offering consultation and professional advice sent to various parts of the country.

These results are not the only outcomes of applying my formula. Once I understood how it facilitated my writing energy, I became curious about its potential in other areas where I had struggled. The tentativeness and timidity that had hindered me in nearly every aspect of my life vanished. Interviews, lectures, and commitments that I had forced upon myself, going against the grain every minute, transformed into enjoyable experiences. Conversely, a dozen trivial self-exploitations that I had allowed—almost as a form of penance—during my deadlock came to an abrupt end. I was finally on good terms with myself, no longer punishing, exhorting, ruthlessly driving myself, and consequently, not subjecting myself to unnecessary boredom and fatigue.

Despite the remarkable success of my formula, I shared it with very few friends. In my almost egotistical belief, shared with most of my peers, I thought my situation was unique—no one had ever fallen into such a state of ineffectiveness before, and no one else could apply my formula to their own challenges successfully. Occasionally, as I was no longer living in a constant state of siege that blinded me to the world outside, I did notice signs that others were wasting their lives similarly to how I had wasted mine.

However, I believed, like me, they would emerge in due course. It was only by chance that I considered publicly offering the simple program that had aided me. Otherwise, I might never have realized that, to a greater or lesser extent, most adults are living inadequate lives and suffering as a consequence.

Several months ago, I was invited to lecture to a group of book-sellers, with the tentative subject being "The Difficulties of Becoming a Writer." In my first book, I had thoroughly explored these difficulties, and I had no interest in simply reciting a chapter from a previously published work. As I began preparing the lecture, I could think of nothing more to add than to candidly state that the most challenging task for a writer is learning to counteract their own inertia and cowardice. Initially fearing that my talk might sound like "testifying to grace" in an old-fashioned prayer meeting, I delved into the subject to prepare my speech.

The conclusions I reached are presented in this book: that we fall prey to a Will to Fail, and unless we recognize it in time and take action against it, we perish without achieving our intentions. There exists a method to counteract this Will, producing results that appear almost magical. I delivered my lecture, and what truly surprised me was the reception. Prior to receiving notes, letters, and phone calls, I had assumed that sharing how one person overcame a dilemma might mildly interest many in the audience and assist a few who found themselves in a similar predicament.

However, it turned out that nearly everyone in my audience was in the state I had described, all seeking help to escape it. I gave the lecture two more times, and the outcomes remained consistent. I was inundated with messages, questions, and interview requests. Most rewarding were three reports I received within two weeks. Three audience members hadn't waited for a more detailed explanation or assumed the formula wouldn't work for them; they immediately put it into practice. One person had written and sold a story that had haunted her for years, dismissed as too "extraordinary" to sell. Another had returned home, putting an end to the exploitation by a temperamental sister, and resumed evening work in a field abandoned at the sister's insistence. Surprisingly, once his sister understood that he refused to be handicapped any longer, she seemed to awaken from a period of peevish hypochondria and became happier than she had been in years. The third case, too personal to recount here, was in many ways the most compelling. At least three individuals, like me, found the formula effective, and each found something awe-inspiring about the results.

We often live well below the potential level for our lives. When freed from the things that hinder us, allowing us to approach our inherent potentialities, we feel entirely transfigured. It is in comparison to the halting, tentative lives we allow ourselves that our rightful full, normal life seems supernormal. Once this is realized, it becomes evident that individuals leading effective lives, be they statesmen, philosophers, artists, or businesspeople, use the same mental attitude, sometimes entirely unconsciously, to carry out their work. Occasionally, as seen in biographies and autobiographies, enlightenment comes through religion, philosophy, or whole-hearted admiration for another. These individuals, even while feeling weak, are sustained by their devotion and capable of feats that astonish us. However, those not born with this knowledge or who do not learn it early on can still teach themselves, through conscious effort, to get the best from their lives. As they do so, many other previously puzzling aspects become clear. This book, however, is not a history of an idea's growth; it is intended to be a practical handbook for those who wish to escape futility and embark on a life of happiness and well-being.

☆☆☆

Why Do We Fail?

With the time and energy we invest in ensuring failure, we could have guaranteed success. A seemingly paradoxical statement? No, fortunately, it is a straightforward, literal truth that holds great promise. Imagine a man with an appointment a hundred miles north of his home, and attending it ensures he would have good health, much happiness, and fair prosperity for the rest of his life. He has just enough time to get there and sufficient gas in his car. He sets out but decides it would be more enjoyable to go twenty-five miles south before earnestly starting the journey. Is that not nonsense? Yes, indeed. The gas had no influence; time had no preference on how it should be spent; the road extended both north and south, yet he missed his appointment. Now, if that man were to tell us he quite enjoyed the drive in the wrong direction, that in some ways, driving with no objective was more pleasant than keeping a date, and that he had a touching glimpse of his old home by driving south, would we praise him for being properly philosophical about losing his opportunity? No, we would consider him foolish. Even if he missed his appointment by getting lost in a daydream and drove past a road sign or two, we would not absolve him. Or if he arrived too late because he lost his way when he could have consulted a good map but failed to do so before starting, we might empathize with him, but we would still criticize his poor judgment.

Yet when it comes to adhering to the appointments we make with ourselves and our own fulfillment, we often behave like the protagonist in this absurd fable; we drive in the wrong direction. We fail where we could have succeeded by expending the same power and time. Failure signifies that energy has been channeled into the wrong direction. It takes energy to fail. This is something we seldom recognize immediately. Because we typically view failure as the conventional opposite of success, we persist in creating false dichotomies between the qualities associated with success and failure. Success is considered invigorating, active, and alert; therefore, the presumed attitude of failure must be lethargy, inertia, a supine position. While this holds some truth, it does not imply that no energy is being utilized. Let any psychologist inform you of the amount of energy a mature man must exert to resist motion. A formidable struggle must be waged against the forces of life and movement to remain inert, although this struggle occurs beneath the surface of our lives, often escaping our awareness. Physical inaction does not truly indicate that life-force is not being expended. Even the idler is consuming fuel while dreaming.

When failure results from dedicating valuable hours to time-consuming pursuits, it's evident that energy is being redirected from its intended course. However, some methods of killing time may not appear as dissipation. They can, on the contrary, seem like diligent and dutiful hard work, earning praise and approval from onlookers and evoking a sense of complacency within us. Only upon closer examination, realizing that this work yields no progress, tires us out, and leaves us unsatisfied, can we understand that energy is once again being channeled into the pursuit of failure.

But why does this happen? If, with the same energy we must expend anyway, we could be succeeding, why do we so rarely lead the lives we envisioned and planned? Why do we achieve so little and irrationally thwart ourselves? Why, when we start late, run out of gas due to carelessness, or miss road signs due to daydreaming, do we think we are being properly philosophical when providing ourselves and others with excuses for failure that won't hold water? No one genuinely consoles themselves by believing that a bird in the hand is worth two in the bush, that traveling hopefully is better than arriving, or that half-a-loaf is better than no bread. Such proverbs are the cynical distillation of experience but are not principles to live by. Our compromises and excuses may be accepted by our peers as long as they are in the same situation, but the successful individual views such whistling in the dark with amusement and incredulity, privately concluding that there is a great deal of hypocrisy in the world. They have firsthand evidence that the rewards of well-directed activity far surpass all the by-products of failure, recognizing that one infinitesimal accomplishment in reality is worth a mountain of dreams.

Even as we speak of the compensations of failure, we are not entirely at ease. Despite our proverbs implying otherwise, we don't genuinely believe that one must choose between success and the good life. We understand that those who succeed experience the same sunsets, breathe the same air, and love and are loved no less than failures. Additionally, they have something more: the knowledge that they have chosen the path of life and growth instead of acquiescing to death and decay. Regardless of how we express ourselves, we acknowledge that Emerson was correct when he wrote, "Success is constitutional; depends on a plus condition of mind and body, on the power of work, on courage."

So why do we fail? Particularly, why do we work hard at failing? Because, alongside being creatures subject to the Will to Live and the Will to Power, we are also driven by another will—the Will to Fail or Die.

When failure results from dedicating valuable hours to time-consuming pursuits, it becomes evident that energy is being redirected from its intended course. However, some methods of killing time may not appear as dissipation. On the contrary, they can seem like diligent and dutiful hard work, earning praise and approval from onlookers and evoking a sense of complacency within us. Only upon closer examination, realizing that this work yields no progress, tires us out, and leaves us unsatisfied, can we understand that energy is once again being channeled into the pursuit of failure.

But why does this happen? If, with the same energy we must expend anyway, we could be succeeding, why do we so rarely lead the lives we envisioned and planned? Why do we achieve so little and irrationally thwart ourselves? Why, when we start late, run out of gas due to carelessness, or miss road signs due to daydreaming, do we think we are being properly philosophical when providing ourselves and others with excuses for failure that won't hold water? No one genuinely consoles themselves by believing that a bird in the hand is worth two in the bush, that traveling hopefully is better than arriving, or that half-a-loaf is better than no bread. Such proverbs are the cynical distillation of experience but are not principles to live by. Our compromises and excuses may be accepted by our peers as long as they are in the same situation, but the successful individual views such whistling in the dark with amusement and incredulity, privately concluding that there is a great deal of hypocrisy in the world. They have firsthand evidence that the rewards of well-directed activity far surpass all the by-products of failure, recognizing that one infinitesimal accomplishment in reality is worth a mountain of dreams.

Even as we speak of the compensations of failure, we are not entirely at ease. Despite our proverbs implying otherwise, we don't genuinely believe that one must choose between success and the good life. We understand that those who succeed experience the same sunsets, breathe the same air, and love and are loved no less than failures. Additionally, they have something more: the knowledge that they have chosen the path of life and growth instead of acquiescing to death and decay. Regardless of how we express ourselves, we acknowledge that Emerson was correct when he wrote, "Success is constitutional; it depends on a plus condition of mind and body, on the power of work, on courage."

So why do we fail? Particularly, why do we work hard at failing? Because, alongside being creatures subject to the Will to Live and the Will to Power, we are also driven by another will—the Will to Fail or Die.

☆☆☆

The Will to Fail

From the disciples of Schopenhauer and Freud, of Nietzsche and Adler, we have all become conversant with phrases such as the Will to Live and the Will to Power. These phrases, representing—sometimes on the verge of overstatement—drives of the organism towards fulfillment and growth, correspond to truths of experience with which each of us is familiar. We have seen children struggle to make themselves and their personalities felt; as young people, we have contended for a chance to try our own emerging forces; after long illness, we have felt the tide of returning strength in our veins. We know that any average person caught in unfortunate circumstances will endure poverty, distress, humiliation, with conditions which an onlooker will sometimes consider as much worse than death; and only the presence of a will to continue living can account for the tenacity with which a person in such circumstances clings to the mere right to breathe and exist.

Furthermore, we first experience and then later turn to realize the process of growth in ourselves. The individual emerges from childhood into adolescence, from adolescence into maturity; and at each of these crises, we find that the activities and interests of the old period are being replaced by those of the new, that Nature is preparing the organism for its new role in the world, is actually reconciling us to the new demands on us by showing us pleasures and rewards in the oncoming state which will replace those we must abandon.

But the idea of another will, a counterbalancing will, the Will to Fail, the Will to Death, is not so readily accepted. For a while, it was one of the tenets of psycho-analysis, for instance, that no individual could actually imaginatively encompass the idea that he might cease to be. Even the death-dreams and suicide-threats of deeply morbid patients were held to be grounded solely in ideas of revenge: the explanation was that the patient thought of himself as living on, invisible, but able to see the remorse and regret caused by his death in those by whom he thought himself ill-treated.

Freud, indeed, analyzing shell-shocked patients after the War, issued a monograph in which he stated that he had occasionally found dreams that indicated sincere death-wishes. This monograph is full of some of the best of Freud's speculations and suggestions; but as for the appearance in popular psychologies of the idea that there could logically be a deathward current running through our lives, it is as though the thesis had never been suggested.

Yet death is as much a fact of experience as birth and growth; and if Nature prepares us for each new phase of life by closing off old desires and opening new vistas, it does not seem too difficult to think that we are, always, being slowly, gently reconciled to our eventual relinquishment of all we hold dear as living creatures. And withdrawal from struggle, abandonment of effort, releasing of desire and ambition would be normal movements in an organism that was being gently wooed away from its preoccupation with life.

It is for this reason that we are entitled to look upon the Will to Fail as a reality. Now, if inertia, timorousness, substitute activity, effortless effort, quiescence, and resignation were found only at the end of life, or when we were drained by sickness or fatigue, if they never handicapped us when we should be in the full flood of our vital powers, there would be no reason at all for attacking this Will to Fail as if it were—as indeed it is—the arch-enemy of all that is good and effective in us. But when it appears in youth or full maturity, it is as symptomatic of something wrong—deeply, internally wrong—with one's life as untimely drowsiness is symptomatic of ordinary bodily ill health.

And if it were easily seen for the black-hearted villain it is when it arrives out of its due time, it would be easy to fight. But almost always we are well within its power before we do more than suspect rarely and vaguely that all is not as it should be with us. We are so accustomed to speak of failure, frustration, timidity, as negative things, that it is like being invited to fight windmills when we are urged to fight the symptoms of failure.

In youth, we seldom recognize the symptoms in ourselves. We explain our reluctance to getting started as the natural timidity of the tyro; but the reluctance stays, the years go, and we wake in dismay to find that what was once a charming youthful diffidence in us is now something quite different, sickly and repellent. Or we find a convenient domestic situation to bear the brunt of excusing us for never having got to work in earnest. We could not leave this or that relative lonely and defenseless. Then the family grows, scatters, and we are left alone, the substitute activity at which we had been so busy is taken remorselessly away from us, and we are sick and terrified at the idea of turning back to take up the long-abandoned plans.

Or we have the best of all reasons for not doing as well as we might. Most of us are under the necessity of choosing between work and starvation, and the employment we were able to find when it was imperative that we should begin earning is not work for which we are ideally suited. When marriage and the raising of a family have been undertaken, the necessity is all the more urgent. We might be willing to wait through a few thin years if no one but ourselves would suffer, but to ask others to do so takes more selfishness, and more courage, than most of us can muster.

Especially in America, where marriages for love are the rule, most young people start out on their married life with little more than their health, youth, and intelligence as capital. We are accustomed to think of the European idea of asking a dot, a dower, from the bride's family as somehow ignoble and mercenary. Yet insisting on that little reserve fund of money with which to meet the demands of establishing a new household has much to recommend it, and the fact that we have no such custom in this country may be one reason why America, the much-vaunted Land of Opportunity, can show so many men and women of middle age wasting themselves in drudgery, filling positions that bring them no joy, and looking forward to a future which at its happiest promises years of monotony, and at its worst the nightmare of poverty-ridden unemployment.

The need to settle for the first job available is sufficient to explain why so few of us actually bring our plans to fruition. Initially, we may have a strong intention not to lose sight of our real goals, even though we must make a living through unpleasant work. We plan to keep our ambitions in focus and work on them diligently, be it during evenings, weekends, or vacations. However, the nine-to-five job is both tiring and demanding; it requires extraordinary strength of character to persevere when the rest of the world is at leisure, especially without any evidence of guaranteed success. Unbeknownst to us, we are gradually pulled into the current of the Will to Fail. We keep moving, unaware that our motion is downstream.

Many of us successfully mask our failures in public, effectively concealing them from ourselves. It is easy to overlook the fact that we are doing much less than our capabilities allow, achieving very little of what we modestly planned to accomplish by a certain age, and probably never attaining all that we had hoped for. One reason for this self-deception is the unspoken agreement we seem to make with our friends and acquaintances along the way. We tacitly plea, "Don't bring up my failures, and I will refrain from mentioning any shortcomings I observe in you."

This discreet silence is rarely broken in youth or early middle years. During this period, the expectation is that at any moment, we may hit our stride. As time goes on, the silence is gradually eased. There comes a point when it is deemed safe to smile wryly and confess that the expectations we had when entering the world were overly optimistic, particularly those related to our own achievements. In the fifties—and sometimes even earlier—it becomes relatively safe to engage in some self-deprecating and semi-humorous grumbling; after all, few of our contemporaries are in a position to say, "Why not start now?" Nevertheless, some of the most remarkable work in the world, including many irreplaceable masterpieces, was created by individuals well past what we superficially consider their prime.

We navigate through the world, failing to contribute, not discovering our full potential, and utilizing only a fraction of our inherent or acquired abilities. If we attain some comfort, garner respect, admiration, a taste of authority, and love, we consider it a good deal, accepting the Will to Fail. We even take pride in our cunning, unaware of the extent to which we've been deceived—settling for the compensations of death rather than the rewards of life.

If the intricate game we play with ourselves and others never concluded, if it never paused for a moment, allowing us to see that it was just a game, the Will to Fail might gently guide us downhill until we settled at its foot, and nobody would object. However, the game has a tendency to abruptly halt, often at its most engaging point. Suddenly, we question why we are caught up in this frantic pursuit, playing hide-and-seek as if our lives depended on it. We wonder what happened to the real life we intended to lead while we were idle or busy with work that only provides us with our basic needs.

Sometimes, the moment passes, forgotten until much later, if ever remembered at all. But for some, it remains unforgettable. If we continue the game, it transforms into a nightmare, and our entire focus becomes how to awaken from it and return to reality. Occasionally, the nightmare seems to intensify; we attempt various paths that appear to lead to freedom, only to find ourselves back in the middle of Alice's Looking-Glass Garden, restarting the hunt once more.

Nevertheless, there is an escape, much like Alice, seemingly going backward initially: by acknowledging the existence of a real Will to Fail and, subsequently, considering ourselves as its victims.

☆☆☆

Victims of the Will to Fail

If the Will to Fail were to declare its presence with symptoms as clear and unmistakable as those of measles or a bad cold, it might have been eradicated or a technique to combat it developed long ago. Unfortunately, its symptoms are diverse and numerous. If you were to pull a dining, dancing, theatre-loving middle-aged metropolitan playboy away from his whirlwind life and introduce him to an unshaven, poorly dressed philosopher daydreaming in the sun, saying, "I want you two to know each other; you have so much in common," you would be deemed mad, yet you would be correct. The daydreamer, the introvert, and the extroverted dancer—at opposite ends of worldly circumstances—are driven by the same impulse; unconsciously, they are both attempting to fail.

Their lives share a common denominator. "Do not act as if you had a thousand years to live," Marcus Aurelius warned himself in his maxims. Those in the grip of the Will to Fail act as if they had a thousand years ahead of them. Whether they dream or dance, they spend their precious hours as though the store of them were inexhaustible.

However, since there are as many ways of failing as there are divisions and subdivisions of psychological types, we often fail to recognize the presence of the Will to Fail in others or ourselves. Here are a few of the innumerable ways of "acting as though you had a thousand years to live":

For instance, there are those who sleep from two to six hours a day more than necessary for perfect physical health. In any individual case, unless the sleeping hours far exceed the normal quota, it is challenging to determine if one is dealing with merely an unusually long sleeper. However, when the note of compulsion enters, one can be certain of encountering a true victim of failure. Those who become irritable or only half alive if an early bedtime is postponed, those who anxiously count each morning the exact number of hours spent in sleep the night before, mourning any interruption, every hour of insomnia, every untimely doorbell, are seeking more from sleep than its normal restorative function. When an adult extends even this, making a daily nap or two routine, the diagnosis becomes straightforward.

Next, among the inconspicuous failures, the "introverts," are the waking sleepers: individuals who let activities pass before them almost without participation or engage in time-killing pursuits where they play only minor and unconstructive roles—the solitaire players, the pathological bookworms, the endless crossword puzzlers, the jigsaw puzzle contingent. The line between recreation and obsession is clear once we recognize its existence.

Easiest to recognize as lovers of failure are the heavy drinkers. A volume could be written on them, but too many volumes have. Where drinking is so constant as to induce a waking sleep or, deeper, a kind of death in life, the presence of the Will to Fail is obvious to any observer. But there are thousands who show the symptoms in so faint a form that they pass almost unnoticed: all those who drink knowing that it means a bad morning the next day, a vague and woolly approach to every problem until the effects have passed off; those to whom any drinking means physical discomfort, whether acute or trifling. Anyone who has learned to expect these consequences and yet continues to expose themselves to them stands convicted of the desire to handicap themselves, at least to that extent. It makes very little difference what the drink in question may be. If coffee disturbs you, if you cannot digest milk, and you nevertheless continue to drink it, you may escape the disapproval meted out to the highball drinker, but you are in the same class. And, plainly, unwise eating comes under the same head.

Turning to the active type, it may be said that the extroverts who pursue failure as their primary career find so many ways of doing it that attempting to tabulate them all would be hopeless.

But, as examples, there are the relentless movie- and theatre-goers, the nightly dancers, all those who count the day lost which has not a tea or dinner or cocktail party in it. . . . No, of course, there is nothing against relaxation and recreation when they are genuinely called for, after a period of contributory activity. But those who object to this classification too early and too angrily, claiming that one must have recreation, give themselves away as setting an abnormal value on release.

Then there are the half-and-half failures, challenging to place, such as the embroiderers and knitters, although it is only fair to say here that sometimes a light task calling for only manual dexterity may go on while the mind is usefully engaged in solving a real problem. Complete honesty with oneself is all that is necessary to discover whether the rhythmical activity is being used in one way or the other. If a dull stupor sets in, or if, on the other hand, the work is just elaborate enough, calls for just enough conscious attention so that no automatic rhythm can be established, then it is rare indeed that this kind of motion can be put in the category of true creative activity, or that of being accessory to creative action.

As for aimless conversationalists, it is easier to see that others fall into that group than to recognize it in ourselves. Sometimes we are startled into realizing that we have repeated the same anecdote to the same friend, and for a few days, we go warily. That is a minor slip. No reminiscent ring, no forced smile on our auditor's lips will stop us when we are habitually marking time with words—when we have the same unevolving round of topics, the same opinions to repeat mechanically, the same half-aimless observations to make on the same recurring situations, the same automatic indignation at the same old abuses, the same illustrations to prove the same points, and a few lukewarm arguments to bolster up what may once have been opinions but are now seldom more than prejudices.

Sometimes, we ride a verbal mannerism so persistently that a listener objects irritably. (Suggestions for overcoming such mannerisms will be provided later; here, we are only considering the way in which they unconsciously reveal the presence of a Will to Fail.) It is probably a stroke of luck to provoke a friend to this extent. If you suddenly discover that you consistently say "I mean," "Of course," "I imagine," "Do you see?" "You know," "As a matter of fact," you are likely to scrutinize your own voice for a period and realize that not only do these tag-words occur repeatedly in your conversation, but there is nothing particularly fresh or valuable about the ideas they have served to embellish. Here, as in the other categories, it is easy to see that something is amiss when encountering extreme examples of the difficulty; an hysterical talker is evidently mentally ill. However, the awareness of subtler forms of the same problem, often concealed for years due to repeating to ever-changing audiences, seldom dawns on us.

There are still more obscure and inconspicuous ways of falling victim to the Will to Fail, ways to which introverts and extroverts are almost equally susceptible. Consider the numerous individuals, for instance, who deliberately undertake work that only requires a small part of their abilities and training, and then drive themselves relentlessly, exhausting over useless details. There are perpetual post-graduate course attendees, appearing on the campus year after year like so many Flying Dutchmen. There are the "devoted" daughters, sons, mothers, and wives (fathers are seldom found here, for some reason, although there may be an occasional husband) who pour their lives into the lives of other adults, but their offering, lacking the true development of what was most valuable in themselves, adds no richness and only insignificant comfort to the objects of their "self-sacrifice." There are those who undertake a task known to be beyond their powers or engage in a specious "research" problem: for example, a man in New York has been collecting biographical details about an obscure Italian statesman since his sophomore year in college. This pseudo-biographer is now in his late forties, and not one word of that definitive Life has been written.

Perhaps the most extensive category of all those whose aim is failure is that of the Universal Charmers.

When you encounter more charm than the situation warrants, it's safe to say to yourself, "Ah, a failure!" This is not a critique of genuine warmheartedness, friendliness, or true sweetness of character. We are now discussing the Harold Skimpoles of the world, the cajoling, winsome adults, whether man or woman, who insist on being perceived by their contemporaries as just a great, big, delightful child—irresponsible, perhaps, not very thoughtful, but exceedingly lovable, even to strangers! There are whimsical teasers and humorous complainers, and if they are good-looking, quick-witted, or amusing, they are more likely than not to succeed in evoking momentary indulgence and tolerant tenderness. It is only in retrospect that one realizes there was no valid reason for the moment's emotion. A healthy adult does not require the tenderness or indulgence of every casual acquaintance. Except for a guilty conscience, no one would ever think of eliciting this kind of response. These victims are under the hard necessity of working at charm as convicts work at stone-crushing; they must continue to be more and more charming to offset their waning attractions or face the truth—admit that they have not adequately fulfilled their responsibilities. As long as their inadequacy is only seen mirrored in the indulgent eyes of another, they can go on without acknowledging the fact that they are failing. So on they go, deceiving their way through life—unless, by good fortune, they can come to see who truly suffers most from the exercise of their charm.

So there are all these ways, and innumerable others, of filling one's time with seemingly purposeless activity or a falsely purposeful routine, and they are all the result of submitting to the Will to Fail. Remember, these activities are only seemingly purposeless. In every case, there is a deep intention, which may be stated in many ways.

We may say that the most obvious intention is to beguile the world into believing that we are living up to our fullest capacity. This is particularly true in cases where the outward life is filled with a thousand trivial matters or one big job of drudgery conscientiously done. Surely, no one could ask us to do more than we are doing! Are we not plainly so busy that we have not one minute or a grain of strength to do anything more? Is it not our duty to do the dull, insignificant, unsatisfying task thoroughly? These are questions that only the individual can honestly answer for themselves, usually in the hours of insomnia or convalescence when the mind, usually engrossed in trivial affairs, finds time to stop and consider. In the long run, it makes little difference how cleverly others are deceived; if we are not doing what we are best equipped to do, or doing well what we have undertaken as our personal contribution to the world's work, at least through an earnestly pursued avocation, there will be a core of unhappiness in our lives that becomes more and more difficult to ignore as the years pass.

The fritterers and players and the drudging workers are mainly focused on deceiving themselves, on occupying every nook and cranny of their waking hours so that there is no room for a hint of futility to seep through. And at night, of course, they are either still engrossed in play or too exhausted to contemplate realities. Yet, when these victims are plainly seen, they present a dreadful spectacle—like insane misers, stuffing a senseless accumulation of trash, odds and ends of sensations, experiences, fads and enthusiasms, synthetic emotions, into the priceless coffer of their one irreplaceable lifetime.

Whatever the ostensible purpose may be, it is evident that one motive is at work in all these cases: the intention, often unconscious, to fill life so full of secondary activities or substitute activities that there will be no time to perform the best work of which one is capable. The intention, in short, is to fail.

☆☆☆

The Rewards of Failure

Absurd as it may seem at first consideration that anyone would solemnly enter into even an unconscious conspiracy to fail, it is a matter of observation that there is hardly one person in a hundred who does not, in some fashion, deliberately cripple and thwart himself. To understand why this should be so, it is necessary to examine, for a chapter, what may be called, without paradox, the rewards of failure.

The recent widespread interest in all branches of psychology has accustomed us to accepting an idea which, when first offered, seemed laughable: that we are all, at some level, engaged most of the time in revery. We dream either consciously or unconsciously, awake or asleep, of a situation in which we feel we should be happier than we are in real life. Occasionally, some childish idea of happiness or success crops up to confuse or hamper us in the business of adult living. Sometimes the dream is of a life of luxurious idleness, the childish Unconscious determined on refusing to leave the safe shelter of the nursery, where all wants were remedied as soon as felt, where warmth and food and love were given freely and unearned. As Emerson wrote, long before we had any technical vocabulary to express that backward-turning revery, long before we knew of "fixations" or of "narcissism," "We do not believe there is any force today to rival or recreate that beautiful Yesterday. We linger in the ruins of the old tent where once we had bread and shelter." To some extent, this is true of all of us, but less true of the happy and successful adult than of others.

At other times, ludicrously enough, the life-wasting revery is about success: the mild man is a Napoleon of war or finance, the mouse-like woman a siren. If reality never broke in upon such revery, the dreamer might be happier, self-absorbed in his silent tale-spinning, than if he were to find himself in a position to realize some part of it. Such revery is in itself compensation for a life of dull routine or uneventful monotony. But, the world being what it is, the dreamer must live, for part of his time at least, in the cold atmosphere of fact. This is no Land of Cockaigne that we inhabit: roast pigs do not run about crying "Eat me!" Fruit does not fall from the trees into our mouths. However blissful the daydream we entertain, we must wake from it sometimes and struggle with the hard conditions of real living.

The inveterate dreamer will struggle only just as much as he needs, and no more. He will do anything half-heartedly to get his bread and butter. Then, when his daily task is over, he will be back at his dreams again, whether he realizes it or not. He succeeds at only one thing: in clearing away a little space, gaining each day a few hours of free time, for just one purpose—to go on wasting his life. But his dream is happy. It is, for him, a true compensation for his failure in every other relation, and so he continues in it. Yet, since after all happiness is the true goal, he is deluded by not realizing that the smallest success in reality brings with it more happiness than years of revery.

Nevertheless, it is important to remember that the rewards of failure are real in their own sphere, for otherwise, we will not brace ourselves to fight them adequately; and there are other rewards of failure besides dreams.

Consider, for instance, that if you try for anything just enough to give yourself some justification for saying that you have tried, you can fold your hands for the rest of your days. You can humbly declare that you were tried and found wanting in those qualities that contribute to real success. This is a rather rare admission, occasionally heard from older failures, usually in a humorously deprecating tone. It sounds very honest and touching, and there is no earthly way to prove against the complainant that his statement is not entirely true. Nevertheless, he has spared himself a lifetime of effort in some way. If you join this group, you can observe the struggles of others with an eye that is half-amused and half-envious, enjoying the results of their successes, but perhaps even more—given human nature—the spectacle of those who fail and take up positions as onlookers beside you.

Then, "Mankind is very superficial and dastardly," as Franklin said. "They begin upon a thing, but meeting with a difficulty, they fly from it discouraged"; and why not, asks the Unconscious, when you can try, stop, and feel for the rest of your life that if you had tried just once more, you would have made the grade? You can thereby become a dilettante or amateur, frightfully hard to please by those who continue working—severest of all critics, either professional or unprofessional, possessor of some inner knowledge, and able to hint at standards of excellence untouched by those still striving in the dusty race; standards so marvelous and unattainable that failure to reach them is more honorable, you may imply, than another man's easy success. With not one thing completed, the acclaim you might have received, the enormous financial coup you might have executed, the masterpiece you might have achieved, can assume in your reverie, and in the eyes of those who accept your version of things, almost more importance than the real success would have had.

Or you can become an abettor and sustainer of more persistent workers and artists, and perhaps that is the friendliest failure, the most successful failure, of all.

But notice that in all these cases, you will, at the very least, have avoided the struggle, the pain, the humiliations that attend outward activity. You will never have to see the object you slaved to bring into being despised or misunderstood. You will never have to feel the rancor of those whom you necessarily surpassed in competition; you will never have to endure the cut of adverse criticism. You will never have to become aware of the malice of those who envy any success, however trivial. You will never have to back your opinions by argument when you are tired and would rather rest for new effort. Or, far deeper and more vital pain, you will never see the discrepancy between the finished work you can do and the work as you had hoped to do it. There is always that discrepancy to keep the honest worker truly humble.

These matters of discomfort and pain evaded are important to notice because when we examine the reasons why we often choose to fail instead of succeeding, they will prove very illuminating. So it is worth understanding that if you fail, you are rewarded by not running the risk of getting hot, tired, discouraged, or sharp-tempered when your co-workers or your materials, whatever they are, seem more refractory than usual. If someone else excels in the line you had dreamed of for yourself, you can always believe that, if you had really tried again, you could have surpassed him.

And then, if you can remain inconspicuous, you will not have the experience of outstripping someone you love. This is perhaps most commonly the woman's Reward of Failure, although the children of distinguished parents or the disciples of outmoded masters in any line also know it. Still, it is only right to say that many who dread the experience of causing pain to another are never called upon to meet it; they failed to take into account the generosity of love. So it is often an excuse for not working that is at the root of this inaction, too, not a real matter of compromising with ambition to keep a vital relationship unspoiled.

By failing, one escapes much gossip and incomprehension, the semi-scandalous talk that most often springs up about those who succeed. To dread this immoderately is neurotic, but this dread does often act as a deterrent to many successes. All vital persons are the target of the curiosity of those who are not vital; but the few whose opinions concern you will know the truth, and the others are of no importance. Yet many withdraw from active life, not to take up an intenser inner life, but merely to avoid the vulgar curiosity of the crowd.

And then, if you have failed not too awkwardly, you are usually more delightful as a companion than a better worker. Those who reach real success are likely to be constant workers. Even in their hours of recreation, they are frequently preoccupied with some element of the thing they are engaged in doing. The successful man has less free time and observes more punctiliously his self-set hours for withdrawing from companionship than the failure. He can seldom be counted on for impromptu gaieties since he is not unconsciously intent on finding any escape at all from the unsatisfactory conditions of his life. And since he has none of the deep interior guilt that haunts the one who knows he is failing, he is under no compulsion to be winning. He reserves his humor and charm, his emotion and indulgence, for those whose lives are closely bound up with his by his own choice. So, except among his real intimates, he may have the name of being gruff and unapproachable or too coolly civil. As long as you cannot bear the notion that there is a creature under heaven who can regard you with an indifferent, an amused or hostile eye, you will probably see to it that you continue to fail with the utmost charm.

Perhaps it will be helpful to look for a while at three lives in which the Will to Fail was at work. In every case, the onlooker would see a life of considerable activity, such obvious activity that he would, at first glance, be likely to agree with the victims that they were in the grip of a perverse fate. On closer examination, each failure will be seen to be by no means determined by any factor outside the individual character. Each of these persons had within himself or herself the abilities necessary to make a full, happy, productive life; each spent what energy he had on defeating his ostensible intention: one saw her mistake and rectified it, one died without facing the truth about his wasted talents. The third is still struggling with his problem, as far from success as ever, though his name is well known.

Case 1 is that of a woman, left a widow while she was still very young. She came from a scholarly family and had been a brilliant student at college. With the little money left to care for herself and her small daughter, she returned to the campus to take degrees as Master of Arts and Doctor of Philosophy in preparation for a career as an educator. Actually (as she found, to her astonishment when her difficulties became so great as to force her to seek advice) she delighted in being a student again, in continuing to live in the condition of a child in an adult world, and therefore strung out her period of preparation as long as she dared. After her Ph.D. was earned, she made what looked to herself and her friends like a good honest effort to find a suitable niche for herself. Only she invariably engaged in wrangling acrimoniously with those who would have to be her superiors, and always about some rather remarkable and original economic ideas of her own. These ideas had nothing whatever to do with the subject she was to teach; their acceptance or rejection by the entire world would not have made one grain of difference in the classroom work which she was called on to perform; but by making an issue of having her absurd and quixotic ideas taken seriously by her co-workers, she brought about—each time she found a position—a situation in which she was distinctly disliked by the very persons on whose goodwill she was dependent.

She went from one post to another, never holding one longer than the year for which she had contracted. She was a good teacher, a well-informed student, and she had much to give, but she carefully saw to it that she would never be in a position to work very hard for very long. Her hopes of a professorship faded. She went from good colleges steadily downgrade to obscure little schools, and as she slipped steadily down, she worked out a philosophy that reconciled her to her steady decline. She held that we all live much too luxuriously and put too high a value on becoming clothes, good food, and comfort. At last, she reached the place where she felt justified in taking an apartment in a tenement district of a large city. Her defiant self-justification broke down, however, when it came to inviting friends to visit her. She grew more and more solitary, more and more eccentric, her running fire of bravado continuing all the while.

Fortunately for her, her one child was a girl, and a girl who grew up to be extremely bright and attractive. She was quite unimpressed by her mother's pseudo-philosophy; she knew that she was being handicapped at every turn by the oddness of their living and dressing, and as she emerged into adolescence she began to fight for a more reasonable life, a suitable background. Matters came to such a pass that either the mother had to take cognizance of the girl's objections or lose her daughter. All the efforts to correct her false position which she made by herself were unavailing. She still brought about the old wrangles whenever possible, she still held the unsatisfactory position to which she had dropped only on tolerance and because she had come to accept a very small salary, in spite of her training and ability.

When at last she sought help from a psychologist, she discovered to her dumbfounded astonishment that she had actually thrown all her energy into failing. Unconsciously she had resented having to go out into the world to work. She wanted to remain either a child or become again a cherished and petted wife. Her wrangles had been, as the analysts say, "over-determined": they were intended partly to make it certain that she would be discharged so that work would become impossible, partly to engage the attention of men. Since she could not acknowledge to herself that she was cold-bloodedly "husband-hunting," she had fallen on the technique—quite as effective in challenging attention as being charming—of starting quarrels. She had a long, hard pull to right the situation she had brought upon herself, but she was eventually successful.

Case 2 is such a one as can be found in almost every town and village in the country, a failure of the sort that is not only treated tenderly but often looked upon as being in some vague way much nobler and finer than any success. It was that of a man with a good mind, noted for his integrity and yet not without a vein of good Yankee ingenuity. He lived and died in the small town of his birth; a rather ugly little manufacturing town. Not because he loved it loyally and wanted nothing better; his reading was always of travel and adventure, and he continually spoke wistfully of countries and places he had never seen. Not that he had no opportunity—opportunity came and tried to hound him into activity. He was the manager of a branch store of a large business, and so satisfactory at it that he was offered a similar position in a larger city, at a correspondingly better salary. He accepted with joy; then within two days he wrote a letter saying that he had reconsidered, that he did not believe that he could fill the better position. His timidity grew on him. A few years later he was combating every improved method that his firm tried to introduce, afraid to try the new ways. A little later he was such an obstructionist that his firm retired him on a minute pension, and he became the town's lovable homespun philosopher.

A senator delivered a moving speech at his funeral, and his fellow townsmen were deeply saddened. It might seem callous to mention that his wife had passed away a decade earlier due to overwork. One son, despite possessing a brilliant mind like his father, only received education from the village school. The other son had to work his way through college, challenging the misconception that working through college is the ideal way to attain education. His daughter sought refuge in a loveless marriage, escaping a home that lacked ordinary comforts.

Let's be clear about one thing: considering honest success as ignoble is either pretense or cant. There is an effort to impose this fallacy, perhaps due to a confusion between the word "success" and the idea of acquiring great fortune through fair or foul means. However, achieving what one sets out to do and receiving rewards, whether in the form of peer approval, the satisfaction of contributing to the world, or fair compensation for valuable services, is not ignoble. This notion is nonsensical and contrary to its claimed "philosophical" nature.

William Ernest Hocking, in his insightful book "Human Nature and Its Remaking," argues, "If command of the fruits of the earth is the normal and destined position for man, why should one who has achieved such a position not receive recognition for succeeding?" He emphasizes that making a fortune is a man's work, showcasing a measure of ability under normal circumstances.

Case 3, a writer and the son of a writer, appears to defy the Will to Fail at first glance. However, despite his fortunate start in the literary world, he lives in constant fear of failure. He avoids work until desperation for money strikes, then writes feverishly until exhaustion, resembling a convalescent afterward. Trying to break this bad habit under a psychiatrist's advice, he attempted to work without urgent financial need, only to produce unacceptable stories that required extensive rewriting. The world remains unaware of these wasted efforts and disheartening revisions, making his career seem drearier with each occurrence and dimming his belief in eventually writing a book he won't be ashamed to sign.

Here again, analysis shed light on the unconscious reason for this action, and once more, the inclination to produce haphazard and unsatisfactory work was overdetermined. On one hand, there was a fear of surpassing his illustrious father in the same profession, and on the other, an unconscious belief that if the stories he seemingly toiled over were rejected, he could avoid working altogether and lead a dream-like life. The Unconscious consistently refuses to grasp the reality that one must consider, refusing to acknowledge that "Work or die" is the rule the average mortal must abide by.

Despite his torment, this man recurrently undergoes an experience that, if comprehended, could show him a way out of his dilemma: when he is finally desperate for money, unable to rely on credit, the indulgence of friends, or his reputation, and has the courage of desperation, he produces material that is immediately accepted. Instead of drawing the workable conclusion from this fact, he has turned it into a superstition, claiming that only work done "at the thirteenth hour" is ever lucky for him. Thus, he continues on his treadmill.

In each of these cases, failure or relative failure brought its reward: escape from adult effort and time to waste in daydreaming. Only in cases where frustration was more painful than success was there an attempt to reshape the life-pattern. Do you not think that those who waste life in this way are at least mildly insane? We all create similar difficulties for ourselves, avoiding work and missing opportunities. Have you ever looked back and thought, "If I had done this or that five years ago, I'd be better off now?" The opportunity was there; why didn't you see it? Are you sure that you are not closing your eyes at this moment to one that you will see later in retrospect? Is the Will to Fail not operating in your own life every day?

Yet the rewards of success are immeasurably more worthwhile. Once more, the smallest task done well, the smallest object out there in the world because of your actions, brings more satisfaction in a moment than failure knows in a lifetime. Knowing that one is being judged by a real scale and not by the shifting standards of reverie is like having solid ground underfoot after weeks of drifting at sea. Only those working on the best they can do are free from the danger of a panic-stricken awakening to reality, an awakening sometimes so late that the very habits and attitudes of normality are forgotten.

Besides the numerous subjective advantages, there are also rich objective rewards. A dream-picture attracts no buyer, a dream-plan yields no dividends, and a fantasized book is followed by no royalty statements. As crass as this may sound in a world that often persuades futilitarians they have chosen the better part, it is the literal truth and represents an even greater truth. Fantasy may label the grapes of reality as sour, but those who have tasted them know a dependable delight at last.

☆☆☆

Righting the Direction

In spite of the Will to Fail, and despite the Rewards of Failure, success remains the normal aim of man, his proper objective. Energy is properly utilized not by expending it to keep ourselves inactive, nor by pushing ourselves into unproductive, sterile activity, but only when it serves the most mature and comprehensive idea of ourselves that we can attain.

The highest idea of success varies from individual to individual and expands with growth. No outsider can dictate another's private definition of success. It may, often does, include recognition from one's peers and greater financial rewards, but it may not. For example, a researcher in the sciences would consider himself fully successful (and rightly so) by contributing one minute fact to the accumulating details guiding scientific progress. His name might remain unknown to those outside his field, and even within it, it could be quite obscure. Nevertheless, he would have achieved his goal if he accomplished what he set out to do.

The success of an actress reaching the pinnacle of her art is on par with that of a mother raising a large and healthy family, but not superior. A priest or minister dedicated to the care of his parish leads a successful life as much as a genius whose name is recognized by many. Others may have an ideal of success that seems incomprehensible to us, but unless we lack imagination, we recognize a successful individual when we see one living responsibly, effectively, usefully, and happily, making the most of their advantages and gifts.

To provide too narrow a definition of success would defeat the purpose of this book. Our skepticism towards the word often stems from not realizing the infinitely extensive range of possible "successes." By late adolescence, each of us has a wealth of self-knowledge, which, if we seriously heed the counsel "Know thyself," could be examined and considered until our ideal of the good life becomes apparent. Education should instill the understanding that every child needs to find this clue to their future and be aware that it can sometimes be muddled by hero-worship or the mistaken belief that an element in one person's success must be present in everyone's success. Despite confusion, false starts, and the adoption of others' ambitions, most of us reach our early twenties with a sense of what we are best suited for or could excel in with the right training and opportunity.

It is crucial to note carefully that unless you have allowed yourself to grossly overestimate your character, your own idea of success is within the realm of achievable goals. Usually, far from overrating our abilities, we often fail to comprehend their true magnitude. The reasons for this underestimation of ourselves will be explored later, but it is essential to recognize that only the truly insane believe themselves suited for careers significantly beyond their capabilities.

The next point to grasp is that in these pages, we are not discussing success of any secondary or metaphorical nature. Your personal idea of success is not here to be replaced by another lofty, "idealistic" compromise. There is no exhortation to lower your hopes and settle for an easily attainable standard. Such approaches merely postpone failure. On the contrary, the more vividly you can envision the original picture of the goal you once aspired to reach, the better your chances of achieving it.

Now, having examined the currents in our nature that lead us to acquiesce in failure, understanding that we can be carried unprotestingly down the path of failure if we allow it to happen, let us explore what is immediately preventing us from making the necessary healthy efforts to succeed.

To do so, we must delve into a subject that is somewhat disreputable today: hypnotism. For various reasons, some valid but others suspiciously weak, hypnotism is seldom studied nowadays. If you have never read a reliable book on the subject, some of the feats claimed for hypnotized persons might seem implausible. However, it's likely that you have come across at least one book on autosuggestion, a method of healing popular about a decade ago, and autosuggestion is a by-product of the nineteenth-century study of hypnotism.

Few contemporary readers are aware of the work of Esdaile in India in the mid-1800s, such as the painless surgical operations he performed on hundreds of patients and his observations on the swift recovery of those who felt no pain during the operation—an early contribution to the theory of the deleterious effects of "surgical shock." The work of Braid and Bernheim is nearly unknown, and Mesmer, who combined a fantastic theory with a mass of remarkably effective experiments, is now primarily regarded as a quack.

There is no doubt that hypnotism is currently discredited, partly because its early practitioners engaged in premature and fantastical theorizing. It also became associated in the public's mind with subjects like "spirit-rappings" and "slate-writing" mediums, many of whom were later revealed as tricksters. Potential experimenters were discouraged from the subject due to unnecessary accompaniments such as hypotheses about "odic fluid" and "animal magnetism"—explanations that clarified nothing. Alongside these prejudicial theories, experiments in anesthesia using chloroform and ether were underway in the same years. Achieving insensitivity to pain through hypnosis was uncertain and presented many challenges: not everyone was hypnotizable, and, more crucially, not every physician could induce hypnosis. Inevitably, the more reliable method of achieving anesthesia through chloroform and ether became widely accepted. The study of hypnotism, once believed by many acute observers of the middle and late nineteenth century to be the initial step toward freeing humanity from physical suffering, as well as overcoming temperamental difficulties and curing vices, declined. With the rise of psychoanalytic theory, the decline of hypnotism, at least for our day, was solidified.

Although the formula we are about to consider doesn't involve autohypnotism, we can still glean insights from this somewhat despised procedure to understand what hinders our effectiveness. Consider the remarkable successes of a good hypnotist with a receptive subject: they seem utterly unnatural, and for that reason, we have not fully understood their potential. For instance, a person typically experiencing vertigo at even a slight elevation can, when hypnotized, walk confidently on a narrow plank at a considerable height. Another individual, seemingly delicate, can effortlessly lift a dead weight. A stammerer, under hypnosis, can deliver a passionate speech without any signs of the speech defect present in their normal state. One remarkable case cited by F. W. H. Myers in his chapter on hypnotism in Human Personality involved a young actress, an understudy suddenly called upon to replace the star of her company, who, sick with apprehension and stage fright, performed competently and brilliantly under light hypnosis, receiving great applause. Yet, it took a while before she could act her parts without the aid of the hypnotist stationed in her dressing room. (In this case, the phenomenon of "post-hypnotic suggestion" began to be observed, laying the foundations for the Nancy School of autosuggestion, with Coué being its most famous contemporary associate.)

In the same chapter where Myers shares the actress's remarkable case, he makes a theoretical observation of immense value to anyone hoping to break free from the bondage of failure. He points out that the ordinary shyness and tentativeness we all experience when approaching novel actions are entirely removed from the hypnotized subject, allowing them to act with precision and self-confidence.

The removal of shyness, known as mauvaise honte, as he wrote, can be achieved through hypnotic suggestion. This process effectively purges the memory by inhibiting the recollection of past failures and freeing up the required set of skills for the moment.

This statement holds a crucial clue, packed with rich implications for those sincerely committed to redirecting their lives toward success. Learning through "trial and error" is often stated as a commonplace. We learn by realizing that one course of action does not lead to the desired outcome; we try again, possibly multiple times, until we discover the procedure that accomplishes our intention. The final step in this series of acts is then adopted.

While this mental picture of the "trial-and-error" method is roughly accurate, it fails to emphasize a key element of the process. Though we may not intentionally focus on it, the Unconscious never forgets the element of pain. We tend to believe, speak, and write as if the one success erases all the failures that preceded it from our minds. However, the importance of the discarded trials ending in failure to our future conduct is tremendous. While we ultimately succeed, we experience failure, ridicule, real pain, and grave humiliation in the interim. Our memories do not solely retain the final success, nor does the success render the failures and pain insignificant to our Unconscious.

The Unconscious fears pain, humiliation, and fatigue, prioritizing the avoidance of pain even more than the pursuit of positive pleasures. Consequently, we often find ourselves succumbing to inactivity and inertia at moments when positive action would be advantageous. Instead of facing the mere possibility of pain, we opt for inaction. To avoid reviving memories of early failures or risking fresh hurts, we unconsciously choose to remain inactive or opt for an easier task.

Sometimes, we initiate a program but retreat quickly when we approach the point where we were previously hurt, finding any excuse to abandon the work unfinished and the reward unclaimed. The childish Unconscious prevails, ensuring that we avoid getting hurt again in an already sensitive spot.

This behavior is utterly illogical. In avoiding trivial discomfort, we accumulate a significant account of failure that may haunt us in the future. We miss countless opportunities that may never come again, subjecting ourselves to far greater pain than the one we manage to evade. Yet, at least the memory of that early humiliation can rest or only stir restlessly, half-awakened.

Now, if that is true—and only a little self-analysis will prove that it is true—how convenient it would be if each of us could carry a hypnotist about, to cast his spell whenever we had to get to work! How marvelous if each of us could have his own private Svengali! Impossible, of course; and, more than that, undesirable. Fortunately, it is not at all necessary to be put under the sway of another's will in order to do our own work. The solution is far simpler. All that is necessary to break the spell of inertia and frustration is this: Act as if it were impossible to fail. That is the talisman, the formula, the command of right-about-face which turns us from failure towards success.

Clear out, by an easy imaginative feat, all the distrusts and timidities, all the fears of looking ridiculous which you may hardly suspect of being treacherous trouble-makers in your life. You will find that if you can imaginatively capture the state of mind which would be yours if you knew you were going towards a pre-arranged and inevitable success, the first result will be a tremendous surge of vitality, of freshness. Then—well, the only way to put it is that it will seem as though your mind gave a great sigh of relief, of gratitude for the liberation, and stretched itself to its fullest extent. This is the moment where one may be forgiven for feeling that there is something truly magical about the whole affair. There will appear an extension of capacity which seems more than normal.

Then the long-dammed-up flow sets in: directly, irresistibly, turned at last in the right direction, the current gathers strength from minute to minute. At first you may still harbor some fear that the spell which worked so instantaneously may break in the same way. It will not, simply because it is no spell; it is a reminder to yourself of the way in which work can always be successfully undertaken. If you remember that, far from your seeing the successful action stop, you will find that each hour of unhampered activity opens out into a promise of others in the future. There may actually be some embarrassment from seeing too many expanding possibilities until you have learned to organize your new life.

Those fears, anxieties, and apprehensions, you see, were far more than mere negative things. By acting as if they were important, you endowed them with importance, you turned them into realities. They became parasitic growths, existing at the expense of everything that is healthy in you. While we allow them to sap us, we are allowing the nourishment which should go towards expanding growth to be used for feeding monsters, cherishing the freaks and by-blows of the mind instead of its extraordinary and creative elements. So that it is not that one is suddenly given wonderful new powers; by ceasing to let fear hold its frustrating sway we come into the use of already existing aptitudes which we formerly had no energy to explore. We discover that we already possess capacities we had not suspected, and the effect, of course, is as though we had just received them. And the rapidity with which these capacities make themselves known when once the aspects are favorable for them is truly somewhat startling. It is even more enjoyable.

Next, there is the further experience of seeming to become, in contrast with one's old self, practically tireless. Actual records of working periods introduced by using this formula would strain the credulity of those who have never yet had the experience. And these periods are not followed by any depressed reaction. There is always so much ahead, and it is so clearly seen, that there is no chance for depression to set in. When the mind is turned back from its onward drive to consider all the tribulations of the past, all the possible mischances which might conceivably happen, it cannot, of course, at the same time explore the road into the future. But once absolve it of the thankless and unnecessary task, and it rewards you by seeming to fly where before it had stumbled and groped.

It takes some self-education to learn how to go from one item of successful work to the next, not to lose time and spend strength—much more happily, but just as surely—in gloating over either the ease with which the task was done or in contemplating too fondly the truly remarkable work one has just been so fortunate as to produce. But a few days' Harvest-Home is quite excusable; and since, still resilient and unexhausted, one looks forward to further activity with enjoyment, there is no permanent danger that the first success under the new régime will be the last.

If you are tempted to look askance at this procedure, to feel that you are being invited to deceive yourself into a feeling of success, you are quite wrong. We are all pragmatists and empiricists in our daily life; what "works" for us is our practical truth, and becomes the basis of our further activity. "Our thoughts become true in proportion as they successfully exert their go-between function," as William James says. And even more fully and convincingly, the late Hans Vaihinger worked out these conceptions in his book, The Philosophy of "As If." Not everyone will go with him to the furthest boundaries of his theory, but it is certainly plain that in most matters of life each of us must act "as if" this or that fact were a self-evident truth. For one thing, if we insisted on proving the reality or efficacy or even probability of most of the conceptions on which we base our practical procedures, we should have no time left in which to act. So, in general, we accept the premises for action which are presented to us on good authority, and use them as proved unless or until our experience causes us to doubt the wisdom of so doing. Then we may reëxamine them and perhaps reach different conclusions from our mentors, but for the most part we all act as if our norms of conduct, our standards of values, were eternally and everywhere valid, so long as they prove practicable for us.

In everyday life, then, if you are ineffectual in your daily encounters and unproductive in your work, you are to that extent acting as if you willed to fail. Turn that attitude inside out, consciously decide that your "As If" shall be healthy and vital, shall be aimed towards accomplishment, and you have made success a truth for yourself. "The law of nature is: Do the thing and you shall have the power; but they who do not do the thing have not the power."

☆☆☆

The System in Operation

If you are the possessor of a very vivid imagination, you will probably be already well on the way towards practice with no more than the clue in that sentence: Act as if it were impossible to fail. If you are not, or if you have been badly hurt by failure, there may be some difficulty in beginning to act effectively, but there need not be very much.

To get at it more slowly, the idea is just this: instead of starting wherever you are—or, to be accurate, instead of trying to start, or swearing that you will start, or deceiving yourself into thinking that you are going to start tomorrow or the day after—beset by all the usual doubts of your performance and memories of past pain, take time first to "make up" your state of mind, the mental condition in which you are going to work.

If you have an important appointment, you do not rush out to it unkempt, unwashed, in any old clothes. You take some trouble to make yourself look as well as you can. Man or woman, you brush and clean your clothes, you look for your good points and emphasize them, you hide or improve your blemishes. Then, when you go to your appointment, you try to act as much as possible as if that heightened condition were your normal state.

Now, you are mentally going to an appointment, an appointment with your successful self. How can you arrange your frame of mind to make that appointment fruitful? You first give yourself a model. Everyone has had a taste of success in some line, perhaps in a very minor matter. Think back to it, however childish it was, even if it was a success of your schooldays. It needn't be, even remotely, success in the adult work you hope to do. What you want to recapture is the state of mind in which you once succeeded. Be careful, now; you do not want to overshoot the mark. Don't jump ahead into the elation which followed the success itself. Just recapture the steady, confident feeling that was yours when you knew the fact that was demanded of you, when you realized that you could do the thing that was necessary, that what you were about to do was well within your powers. Try to bring back as clearly as you can every surrounding circumstance of that moment.

Now transfer in imagination that success-sequence to the work in hand. If you were absolutely certain that everything about the present work would go as smoothly as everything went when you succeeded in the past, if you knew that what you are beginning would certainly go well, from the moment you begin till the moment of the work's ultimate reception, how would you feel? How would you act? What is the state of mind you would be in as you launch out into it?

Fix your attention on that, for that is to be your working frame of mind. Until you can reach it, refuse to begin; but insist on reaching it as soon as possible. When you have found the mood, hold it steadily for a while, as if waiting for a word of command. All at once you will feel a release of energy. You have received from yourself your working-orders, and you can begin. You will see that you no longer have to push yourself to do the work; all your energy is free to push the work alone.

It was the additional, unnecessary effort of pushing aside your own inertia that gave the impression, previously, that you were too hindered to start, fumbling through a fog to reach your goal, or frequently halting to dispel half-realized doubts, anxieties, and memories of failure buzzing around you like a cloud of gnats. Clear all that away before you begin working by simply refusing to entertain the mere possibility of failure.

Afterward, work until you sense the unmistakable onset of true fatigue. True fatigue. The early waning of attention will be merely the old state of mind attempting to creep in once more when your attention is elsewhere. If that happens, pause for a moment and tell yourself, "No. That is the way I will not think!" eradicate the impulse entirely, and continue working. When your muscles and mind genuinely protest that they have accomplished all they should for the time being, pause and find some relaxation. If bound by office hours, quietly retreat alone for a while when the old state of mind seems in danger of returning or when you anticipate spending time adjusting a fellow worker's attitude before smoothly transitioning into the new way. Remain alone until you have re-established your confident attitude, then rejoin the group.

When the time for relaxation arrives, you'll discover that you finally experience the full joy of playing. Some individuals may have been so badly bruised that, although any undue self-indulgence should be avoided, it might be necessary to initially practice this system for only a brief period each day and on some secondary desire. Most educators concur that the optimal way to teach a child to act confidently and competently, and to facilitate the learning process, is to first ask them to perform a small task well within their untrained abilities. As Dorothy Canfield Fisher states in her excellent book for parents and teachers, "Self-Reliance," "Success or failure in adult life depends largely on the energy, courage, and self-reliance with which one tackles the problem of making their dreams come true. Self-confidence in any enterprise usually comes from remembering past success." And, once more, Professor Hocking in "Human Nature and Its Remaking": "Education involves supplying the halted mind with a method of work and some examples of success. There are few more beautiful miracles than leading a despairing child to a trifling success, and there are few difficulties whose principle cannot be embodied in such a simple form that success becomes easy and revealing. By increasing the difficulty in serial stages, the small will, under the cumulative excitement of repeated and mounting success, may find itself far beyond the obstacle that originally hindered it."

In our own experiences, when self-confidence wanes, we should seek out some modest desire that, for whatever reason, has yet to be fulfilled. Opportunities for such endeavors abound in every life. In these attempts towards success, the key is either to transform a dream into reality or to rectify a flawed approach that hinders the desired outcome.

Take the example of the unforgettable Bunker Bean and how his life transformed when a deceitful medium convinced him he was the reincarnation of a Pharaoh. His ascent in the world was swift; success followed success, creating a positive chain reaction. Even after realizing he had been duped, that he was no reincarnation of Rameses, and the sold mummy-case was not an artifact from ancient Egypt, Bunker Bean had mastered the art of success, preventing him from slipping back into obscurity. If you recognize any resemblance to H. T. Webster's Mr. Milquetoast in yourself, revisiting Bunker Bean could prove worthwhile; the time spent won't be in vain, as it's as funny as it is profoundly true.

Consider these instances of cultivating secondary talents to subsequently boost confidence in crucial matters:

In New York, a highly successful psychiatrist recently took up clay modeling, followed by learning the art of coloring and glazing pottery. This venture was a deliberate attempt to gain success in a hobby, given that his profession required constant dealings with challenging subjects. The confidence gained in this pursuit spilled over into his demanding daily work. Additionally, he developed a captivating hobby that rejuvenates his mind, earning him more approval as his modeling became consistently amusing and occasionally distinguished. You might think he possessed considerable talent, but what he truly had was the awareness of his long-standing attraction to the idea of modeling; he only delved into clay when he reached his thirties. He simply transformed a desire shared by almost everyone into a source of pleasure and added self-assurance.

Similarly, at the Art Institute of Chicago, there's a room named after a business man who took up painting after turning fifty. Participating in a competition where his identity was unknown, he won the first prize. Now, there's a club in Chicago comprising middle-aged business and professional men studying art and producing commendable work.

A thirty-year-old clerk in a business office, who lacked early advantages, had harbored a lifelong desire to play the piano. One day, on her walk home, inspired by an impulse she wisely followed, she entered a house advertising music lessons through a small sign in the window. Her success is, of course, relative. She lacks the time required to become an excellent musician, and she didn't commence early enough to train the specialized muscles of a professional pianist. Nevertheless, she achieved her personal goal. That moment of courage transformed her entire life. Transitioning from the overworked and oppressed drudge of her home, she now resides in her small apartment, visits her family with amicable indifference, and has formed a group of friends with aligned tastes. Apart from the joy derived from understanding music as only a performer can, she knows she has acted in an adult fashion, boosting her confidence in every aspect of her life.

These three cases offer a glimpse, at least, of the proper procedure. Take a decisive step to turn a dream into reality. Suppose you've longed to travel but have never had the opportunity. If this dream is to move from the realm of imagination to reality, several essential steps must be taken. If you're neglecting these steps, you're providing evidence that your infantile unconscious is dictating the terms of your life rather than your rational mind. Let's say you aspire to visit Italy. You'll undoubtedly enjoy the experience more if you can speak a few words of the language, read a current newspaper in Italian, or have knowledge of Italy's past. Do you? There are numerous excellent small grammars, phrasebooks, and histories available. How better to start than by quietly purchasing one of these? What else will you need? Time and money. Flip the usual phrase and acknowledge that money is time; if you have funds for travel, you also have a time fund. Begin accumulating it. Set aside a small coin each day, but don't stop there. Consider what work you can do in your spare time to earn extra money for your journey. Even if it's as simple as babysitting during parties, view the payment as wholly dedicated to your travel intention, and you'll be moving towards a successful life.

A young and hard-working assistant editor, desiring to travel, found his way to the offices of an Italian newspaper printed in New York. There, he received assistance in translating an advertisement he had written into Italian, offering lessons in English or journalism in exchange for Italian lessons. Two years later, he went to Italy as a tutor-companion to a young boy. Today, he holds a minor position in the diplomatic service, a goal he always envisioned but had deemed unattainable for years due to living on the financial edge.

Be careful that you do not turn these first steps into merely a more elaborate way of playing the old game of day-dreaming with yourself. Do something every day towards your intention, however remote your goal may have to be. If you like to model, stop at a ten-cent store and buy plasticine tomorrow; if to travel, write for folders; at the very least, if you have no money to spend at all, you can go to, or get into correspondence with, the nearest public library, and learn to use the expert services of librarians.

At first say as little as possible to others of what you intend to do. Get an effect before beginning to talk. If you talk too soon you may almost come to feel that there is a conspiracy against your doing anything out of your usual routine; you will be at least partly right. Those who are still slaves to dreams, to the Will to Fail, are made uncomfortable by the sight of anyone who is breaking free. They feel that there is in the unwonted action some criticism directed at themselves, and become uneasy. At any moment, the Unconscious knows, its supremacy may be disturbed, its opportunities for revery taken away from it. So it begins to fight. One of the most universal forms this combat takes is that of quotation; maxims which sound wise, but which are usually only self-consolatory, spring to the lips of those who reject reality. "The skies change," they will say to you, sententiously; "the heart remains the same," but they will not be quoting in the sense of the original. Or "The grass is always greener on the other side of the fence" you will hear, from those who cannot be bothered to look beyond their own front yards. And so the subtle process of undermining your enthusiasm, and bolstering themselves in their own opinion, will go on. If proverbs fail, they will fall back on teasing.

Now you, if you are at last tearing yourself free, are entering into a conspiracy with Reality, an agreement to see how much may be got out of life if you act with a little more directness and courage than you have used before. Don't put yourself into a position to be discouraged at the start, or bullied out of, or teased about, your new program. Within a short time the results of your action will speak for themselves, providing you with all the justification you need.

Always start by asking yourself, "What would I be doing now if it were genuinely impossible for me to fail at—whatever it is: traveling, modeling, writing, farming?" It could be any of these things, or one of a hundred more: dancing, dress-making, studying calculus or Greek, becoming better looking, or enjoying more music. Whatever it is, with a little thought, you can easily figure out the initial step if you were dealing with reality, not just dreaming of a different life. Now that you're dealing with reality, take that first step. Then ask yourself the next, and so on until you see your ambition taking shape in your life, starting to grow independently and carrying you along effortlessly. "Life is infinitely flexible," as an old analyst used to say to his patients. While that might be a bit extreme, it's true that life is more malleable, more flexible, than it appears when we hesitate to act.

Alternatively, there's another way to start acting successfully. We often underestimate the amount of friction we face in our lives due to expecting rejection or being ignored. Recall an encounter you had today in your office, a store, or with a servant or tradesman in your home. Try to remember the way you made your request. Despite courtesy or respectfulness, was there not a hint of tentativeness in your request? Did you ask for cooperation in a way that allowed room for refusal, grudging action, or being ignored? Now, think about the ideal way that question could have been asked or that order given. It can be just as courteous, but in a way that leaves no room for refusal without being deliberately surly and hostile.

That is the tone of success. When you find it, you not only benefit yourself but also the person you're working with for effectiveness. Don't waste someone else's time, energy, or your own patience by suggesting, even indirectly, that there is more than one course of action when there's only one that will get the result you require. The work takes half the time if the attention is undivided and free to move quickly to the next demand.

Have you ever found yourself in an office where a co-worker, perhaps considering herself a bit too refined for her role, approaches you with a request? "Oh, Mr. Robinson," she may say, with exaggerated politeness, "if you have just a moment to spare, would you mind going over those reports on your desk sometime soon? I hate to trouble such a busy man, but Mr. Smith needs them." Now, whether it's deplorable or not, it's just plain human nature to wish you didn't have a moment to spare, to instinctively look for something else to do that would make you too busy to address that request right away. Yet, in all likelihood, going over those reports is the next item on your agenda. If you succumb to the temptation to delay the work and teach the self-appointed aristocrat a lesson, you end up stalling the entire office workflow and may face consequences from your superiors. Didn't the unfortunate way that simple request was made waste your time and energy? Yet, the odds are, you might make similar requests yourself, inadvertently creating tension and unnecessary formality.

These might seem like minor matters, but it's the accumulation of successfully managed small things that elevates a life beyond the mundane. Women, in particular, may fall into the trap of using the wrong tone with subordinates or office associates, contributing to complaints of discrimination in the workplace. By approaching human interactions with the right attitude, using a tone that is both courteous and firm, you treat others as willing co-workers rather than touchy subordinates.

Before you start your day, take a moment to imagine all the interactions you're likely to have and consider how best to handle them. Listen to your own voice and adjust it until you find a tone that is both polite and assertive. By doing so, you'll find that you navigate your business day with less fatigue, leaving room to fulfill some minor wishes you've secretly harbored. From there, it's just a step towards gathering the courage to tackle the major things you've long wanted to achieve.

☆☆☆

Warnings and Qualifications

Before delving further, it's essential to clarify what this system does not involve. This advice does not advocate hypnotizing yourself into success, a notion that may cause anxiety for many due to the association with hypnotism and self-suggestion. While the Nancy school, popularized by Coué, offers valuable insights into self-management, and Baudouin's book, "Suggestion and Autosuggestion," is worth reading, the widespread fad has diminished. Despite warnings, many attempting self-cure ended up intensifying their initial troubles.

No, despite a connection to a hypnotism-related sentence in a chapter, the association with hypnotism ends there. The recommendation is to employ a minimum of will—just enough to decide to try a new process. Similar to the Nancy school, the imagination takes over until your mind becomes clear, cool, and "pleasant" in tone, not confused, diverted, troubled, or foggy.

The crucial distinction lies here: in intensive autosuggestion, there's a risk that the mind becomes disconnected from reality in the opposite direction as it was in day-dreaming or depression. It might become, as the French say, "exaltée," a term for which there's no exact equivalent, but it roughly implies being "extravagantly elated." This mental intoxication is as dangerous as it is temporarily delightful. You cannot sustain life on those peaks, and even if you could, you would find yourself unable to act effectively in the real world. Without such action, success remains elusive, and self-delusion persists.

What we truly need is confident, steady, freely-flowing action. Only then does safe delight emerge. The mind, free of doubts, expands and relishes its own activity, and the rewards of satisfactory action become apparent. This natural elation, unrelated to delusion or hypnotism, follows and doesn't face later reactions that nullify it.

Secondly, the advice cautions against adopting "affirmations" like "I cannot fail" or "I am successful in all I do." While this approach is beneficial for many, it closely resembles auto-hypnotism for those who lack a thorough understanding of the underlying principle. The philosophy supporting religions that employ "affirmations" is commendable, suggesting an ultimate unity behind the world's duality or diversity. Nevertheless, our conditioning by the flesh, personality, and the concrete world prompts us to act as if the world's constitution were dual, with good and evil evenly distributed. Attempting the "affirmative" method often encounters resistance from prosaic common sense, leaving many feeling ludicrous. Some may succeed briefly only to find themselves worse off later. There's no disapproval for those temperamentally suited to this method, but for even mildly skeptical individuals, it may prove more irritating than helpful.

Thirdly, the advice discourages hastily trying to impress others through posing, pretending, or outright lying about one's success. The initial goal is self-impression, creating a congenial working atmosphere.

The recurring recommendation is simple: Act as if failure were impossible.

Above all, you're not encouraged to indulge in yet another fantasy about success, even if it's more detailed than previous daydreams. However, this fantasy should not bear signs of kinship to your former daydreaming and necessitates a different use of imagination, which merits detailed scrutiny later.

Long before Freud contributed to modern thought, Pico della Mirandola, in a treatise called "De Imaginatione—Concerning the Imagination," discerned two kinds of reverie: one retrograde, hindering a man from his work, prolonging irresponsibility and mental childhood; the other, true imagination, was found in successful individuals. Joubert's aphorism, denying the name of Imagination to the former type of reverie, provides a concise definition: "Fancy," he asserts, "an animal faculty, is very different from imagination, which is intellectual. The former is passive, but the latter is active and creative."

It is the creative imagination, the latter type, that should be summoned. Keeping this fact fully in mind prevents the peril of reverting to the old habit of reshaping the world in dreams while life slips away. Recall once more that "Success depends on a plus condition of mind and body, on power of work, on courage." Hold firmly to the idea that the correctness of dreaming or imagining is tested by subsequent action. Any mental activity turning backward for longer than necessary to correct a mistake or replace an unsatisfactory habit is detrimental and cannot be sustained if a fuller life is the goal.

You predefine the hours during which you will work. Within those hours, as part of the work, you initially clear and free your mind. Once this brings you to a pleasant, confident, and calm state, you are prepared to engage in the actual work. The initial part of the time is spent preparing for action. You clear the decks; you act.

In this age of alibis, where knowledge about Glands Regulating Personality and the Havoc raised by Resistances abounds, the temptation to be lazily distinctive is widespread. While it's true that proper glandular dosage can help many cases of subnormal energy, how many who mention being probably hypo-thyroid* actually undergo a basal metabolism test to confirm the issue? They might argue that the situation is too grave to muster the energy to begin a cure, and there's no response to that. Yet, if lethargy genuinely hampers you, consulting a good diagnostician may be your first step toward success. If necessary, mind you, as a significant fact challenges the talk about glandular insufficiency, often appearing as an alibi. Specialists in glandular therapy would confirm that increasing habitual activity gradually prompts glands to respond with increased secretion. In many cases, starting at the other end can cure this condition. Following this advice will not lead to a subsequent breakdown unless you intentionally (with the intent to cripple yourself) leap from a practically comatose state to one of manic activity.

As for Resistances, they are almost a tenet in the current secular religion. Individuals who wouldn't consider going through the time, expense, or trouble of a full analysis will confidently claim to have "a resistance" to this or that, feeling that admitting their handicap fulfills all that can be asked of them. Noteworthy recoveries from resistances have been observed in those who seriously heeded the advice to replace that term with our ancestors' outdated synonym for the same thing: "bone-laziness." It may not be as enjoyable or flattering to be foolishly lazy as it is to be the victim of a technical term. Still, many are hindered by an impressive word, individuals who would have faced no such trouble in a simpler and less self-indulgent society. Those genuinely, deeply, and unhappily gripped by a neurosis should promptly turn to one of the well-known therapies. Unless one is willing to do so, it should be socially disapproved to technically refer to such difficulties.

If the alibis of the age were in any way generally helpful, if they weren't excuses for remaining inactive, and if inactivity were genuinely a happier state than effectiveness, there would be little harm in indulging in contemporary patter, even without the specialized medical or psychological knowledge necessary for using the terminology correctly. Before concluding that you are the victim of uncooperative glands or a villainous Resistance, try a few suggestions for self-discipline in a later chapter. You might find them so enjoyable, your expanding powers so much more rewarding than—well, your bone-laziness, that you won't need the services of an expert after all.

☆☆☆

On Saving Breath

Earlier in these pages, advice has been given to refrain from talking excessively. It might appear as if I believe that one of the prerequisites for success is to immerse oneself in a surly silence. Nothing could be further from the truth. Talking enough, talking persuasively, and establishing friendly relations with those around us are supremely important for effective living. However, it is easy to talk too much, at the wrong times, or with the wrong objectives. Numerous proverbs highlight the danger of excessive wordiness. We say, "Speech is silver, silence is golden"; "Much talk, little work"; "A barking dog never bites." We describe the tongue as "the unruly member," label a gossip's tongue as "hung in the middle," term a demagogue as "a wind-bag," praise "a man of few words," and sometimes feel uncomfortable witnessing the strength of laconic speech.

Without emphasizing the matter excessively, it's worth examining a few reasons for advocating silence. Every great religious discipline stresses the wisdom of mastering the control of speech. Some Christian sects observe silences, and some commit to perpetual silence. A significant philosophical-religious system, like that of the Indians, dedicates a phase of its training not only to controlling speech but also to controlling breath: the Pranayama of the Hindus. In Latin, the words for breath and soul are masculine and feminine forms of the same root, while in Greek, they are identical.

There is more to this than meets the eye of the reader in a hurry. Breathing is one of the few involuntary actions of the body that we can voluntarily control. In other words, it lies on the border between the realms of the conscious and the unconscious. The individual who can speak or be silent as they choose demonstrates self-control.

When the Unconscious has us fully at its mercy, we speak not as we would voluntarily choose if we could see all the consequences of our speech but from a need to relieve some half-perceived pressure. We humorously grumble about our difficulties, making ourselves self-conscious in the process. Alternatively, we defiantly excuse ourselves or complain of a trifling injustice, sometimes surprised by the excess pity we invoke. Once we discover a wellspring of pity and indulgence in another, we are seldom mature enough not to take advantage of it, thus reinforcing our infantilism and hindering our growth.

One of the most deceptive traps of the Will to Fail is its tendency to make its victim seek unnecessary advice. Once again, the fundamental underlying reason for seeking advice (which, let's emphasize once more, is unnecessary) is that it allows us to maintain a sense of protection and nurturing, even as adults. However, this also means we're given pretexts for failure in advance. If we follow someone else's advice and fail, it's clear that the blame falls on them, not us; isn't that obvious? Thus, we can continue to indulge in fantasies of successful actions, convincing ourselves that if only we had followed our initial instincts, failure wouldn't have been an option.

Considering such motives, it's prudent to examine every urge to seek advice carefully. If the intention behind the desire is unquestionable, then there's only one more question to ponder before seeking assistance with a clear conscience: "If I were to figure this out on my own, would it only consume my own time?" If the answer to that is "Yes," then it's generally preferable to solve the problem independently, unless the time spent doing so would vastly outweigh the importance of the outcome.

For those engaged in creative endeavors, it's important to remember that time invested in developing an independent approach is rarely wasted. We often marvel at the success of individuals like Joseph Conrad, who mastered the English language despite being Polish, or at the achievements of electrical genius Steinmetz. The fact that they had to tackle their challenges alone may seem like a daunting obstacle to overcome, but in reality, this need for independent action was crucial to their success. Recognizing this fact doesn't diminish their accomplishments in any way. Many of us rely heavily on each other's support to the point where our individual contributions are minimal; the end result of our efforts becomes a mixture of various tastes, talents, and techniques, hardly distinguishable from similar outcomes. Just take a moment to examine the typical novels, magazine advertisements, or comic strips produced en masse—they all seem to emanate from some central authority, despite being attributed to different individuals or entities. Yet, we reserve our true admiration for those who bring us something fresh or exhibit genuine genius.

Therefore, the painstaking process of developing an original technique, despite the effort and isolation it may entail, is worthwhile. Keeping this in mind, let's explore when it's appropriate to seek advice.

You're facing a genuine problem. The initial step, therefore, should be to articulate it in writing or verbally with precision, so you can clearly identify what's troubling you. If you allow the problem to swirl around in your mind without formulating it, it will seem much larger and more vague than it actually is upon closer examination. Then, seek out an expert, whether a friend or a stranger, but strive to find someone whose perspectives resonate with you, as this usually indicates similar or compatible thought processes. Doing so earlier will prevent you from wasting both your time and theirs by involving them in only a portion of your self-examination. If you manage to secure a meeting, keep it as brief and concise as possible while still addressing all your concerns. Then, follow the advice you receive until you observe definite results. If you're tempted to dismiss it with "Oh, that won't work for me," you should question your own motives. Such a rejection suggests that you already had a course of action in mind and were secretly hoping to be advised to pursue it. Sometimes, witnessing a negative example of how not to approach advice and instruction can be more enlightening than a positive one.

Have you ever observed an art class teacher in action? Often, when they identify a flaw in one student's drawing that is common among most students at that stage, they'll gather the class around the easel to use the imperfect canvas as a teaching tool. They'll provide criticism, advice, encouragement, and occasionally correct the mistake by erasing lines or adjusting colors. If you pay attention to the group at this moment, you'll notice that everyone seems to benefit from the lesson except the student whose work is being used as an example. In nearly every case, the student whose work is on display appears nervous, sometimes tearful, often angry—in short, exhibiting signs that they feel deeply humiliated and insulted, reacting at a childish level. If you seek help or position yourself in the role of a student to a teacher, learn to progress through your mistakes rather than being overwhelmed by them. Maintain an impersonal attitude while you're being guided back to the correct approach.

If you're in school or receiving class or private instruction, it's wise to seize every opportunity to ask thoughtful questions, then act on the information provided, and finally—and very importantly—report back to your instructor on your success or failure in following their advice. This benefits not only you but also your instructor and future students, as they can't discern which methods are effective and which are only beneficial to them and a select few unless their students provide feedback in this manner. If you consistently report no progress, then one of two things must be true: either you're not fully comprehending the instruction, or you're not under the guidance of the right mentor.

Once your apprenticeship period concludes, try not to undermine yourself or cultivate so much self-doubt that you constantly seek help for minor procedural matters. Every physician and psychiatrist is familiar with a significant group of "patients" who repeatedly return, posing numerous and trivial questions, indicating a level of helplessness that suggests they might never have matured fully if they were as reliant on others in all aspects of life as they appear to be with their physicians. Genuine professionals rarely welcome such patients. Individuals who seek excuses for their failures or refuse to mature and resolve their own difficulties will persist in seeking advice until their final moments, and even the most astute consultant may occasionally mistake an infrequent questioner for one of the weaker types.

A useful litmus test to determine if you're merely indulging a nervous habit of dependency is to ask yourself in each instance: "Would I pose this question if I had to pay a specialist's fee for the answer?" Busy individuals who are frequently in the spotlight receive numerous requests for personal consultations. They typically respond as best they can, often going to great lengths rather than risk discouraging any talented or sensitive novice, but they are often taken advantage of. Occasionally, when a distinguished individual stops entertaining such questions, it's not because of conceit or a lack of willingness to assist those genuinely perplexed, but rather because they struggle to distinguish sincere inquiries from those driven by neuroses. Thus, if they still have their own valuable work to attend to, they reluctantly opt for silence. They console themselves with the understanding that many individuals who are eager to do their own work often hinder themselves by displaying excessive humility, and if their questions remain unanswered, they will eventually find satisfactory solutions on their own.

Therefore, discussing, complaining, seeking advice, and soliciting suggestions are all better left behind during the period of re-education. Ultimately and ideally, you aim to be capable of working under any circumstances. You can never be certain that your favorite confidant or most stimulating friend will always be available to lend a sympathetic ear precisely when you feel the need. Establishing a habit of turning to someone at a specific stage of your work, and even unconsciously convincing yourself that this is necessary for satisfactory performance, sets the stage for future failure.

Furthermore, regardless of your field, if you dedicate every available moment to creative activity, you'll eventually accumulate a body of your own work and a wealth of experience to draw from; you'll develop a "feel" for your material. At that point, you'll realize how many of your problems stemmed from being in the position of an amateur or novice, lacking sufficient experience in your field, which made every problem seem unique for a time.

☆☆☆

The Task of the Imagination

We've already explored the role of imagination in leading a productive life to some extent, and we've relied on it to create a favorable mental atmosphere necessary for producing our best work. However, imagination serves countless other purposes; its applications are so varied that it often seems like a different faculty altogether in each instance.

In everyday life, we often view imagination as something that might be considered "useful" for artists of various kinds, but almost the opposite for practical individuals. Generally, using one's imagination is seen as taking a break, allowing the mind to wander aimlessly, relaxing and idling away. After indulging in it—since we typically perceive exercising the imagination as a form of indulgence—we may return feeling rejuvenated to the ordinary tasks, or we may find that we've wasted time, missed opportunities, fallen out of sync with our peers and allies, and ultimately suffered for giving free rein to one aspect of our mind.

As a result, we often regard imagination with caution, sometimes attempting to suppress it, or in extreme cases, even eliminate it altogether. Many readers may recoil at the notion that imagination can be immensely beneficial in mundane affairs. However, this reluctance stems from viewing imagination as a faculty that always wanders unchecked, needing to make its own rules and occasions, seemingly incapable of being directed, and largely beyond control—unable to serve reason and will. When controlled and directed, though, it becomes the mature creative imagination, the spiritual faculty that Joubert speaks of.

Consider a few of the numerous useful functions it can serve: it can help us detach somewhat from ourselves, keeping our emotions and biases, which often cloud our judgment, under control. By doing so, we may realize that we're consistently acting against our own best interests, and we can replace these disadvantageous behaviors—still within the realm of imagination—with others that lead to more favorable outcomes. We can also apply it to the character of an opponent or an uncooperative "ally," studying them as an author might study a character they intend to include in a book. We can glean insights into their motives and then observe whether our assessments were accurate, thereby avoiding mistakes such as being too abrupt with a sensitive individual or overly indulgent with someone who will take advantage of us if given the chance.

Nor does this even begin to cover all the ways in which imagination, rather than leading us into daydreaming and resignation to unsatisfactory circumstances—or even just serving as a form of entertainment—can contribute to the creation of a fulfilling life. When working as much as possible under the direction of the will and in cooperation with reason, imagination can explore new avenues for our endeavors, reviving some of the original enthusiasm towards our work that we've lost due to fatigue and routine; it can even serve such a profoundly practical purpose as discovering new markets for our products or fresh ways to utilize our existing talents.

These concepts merit closer examination here, and later we'll introduce some exercises on utilizing the imagination.

We need not be part of the group that can only learn through direct experience. Recognizing that much of our apprehension about embarking on new ventures stems from an unvanquished fear of the pain we encountered in the past when we began to progress, we can decide that some of our trial-and-error experiments in managing life will take place in the mind, in the realm of imagination, where they are essentially painless. We can learn to anticipate imaginatively, thereby avoiding mistakes, inefficiency, and wasting energy and time.

Primarily, we can use our imagination to gain perspective on ourselves and our work.

Everyone understands how a child completely identifies themselves with everything they own and do, as well as with those who care for them. They feel outraged if asked to share their possessions; the breaking of a beloved toy is a tragedy; if it rains on the day of a planned picnic, they might feel as though the sun will never shine again. If a mother or caregiver leaves them while they're awake, they feel deeply betrayed. Much of early education aims to teach the young egotist to perceive themselves in a somewhat truer relation to their world. Each of us, to a greater or lesser extent, has had to learn this lesson; however, it's seldom fully comprehended. Even in our later years, traces of childish egotism persist—sometimes so strongly that adults may suffer, resent, sulk, and complain in a manner reminiscent of nursery tantrums.

No success occurs in isolation from others. (The notion of an artist who "works only to please himself" is as mythical as the hippogriff.) Given this reality, there will be occasions when it's immensely important for us to perceive ourselves clearly and in proportion to those around us. At some point, each of us may need to remind ourselves, "Here I am; here is the work I do; here are those I hope to assist and satisfy through this work." Imagination can assist us in stepping back and gaining a perspective on that relationship, analyzing its components, and revealing the full extent of what we've undertaken.

The immature adult is unable to view himself from a distance, let alone perceive his work or creations as they truly are, without being distorted by excessive personal pride or diminished by humility and fear. Consequently, he never truly grasps the extent of his contribution to his world's framework and relies on the feedback of friends or strangers, but even then, he remains confused. Regardless of how straightforward the words or accurate the evaluation may be, he fails to truly listen because he cannot bring his undivided and emotionally detached attention to the moment. His intense preoccupation with his own aspirations and desires makes him a poor judge. He cannot benefit from good advice or sound criticism, nor can he discern when advice is misguided or criticism lacks expertise. By imaginatively examining himself, the work he intends to undertake, the audience he hopes to reach, and then correlating these elements, he could safeguard his confidence, maintain clarity of mind amidst conflicting advice, and accurately assess his performance.

Continuing to excessively identify ourselves with the work we do is a grave error that can harm and hinder us. Recent years have taught us the folly of becoming so enmeshed in our children's lives that they become incapable of living independently. A mother who clings to her adult (or even adolescent) child, suffering alongside him, making decisions for him, enduring humiliation on his behalf, unable to fully live her own life unless he conforms to her expectations, meddling in his affairs, and dictating his professional and social interests, is no longer seen as the epitome of maternal love and wisdom. While we may not always act as wisely as we should, few men and women today view complete self-identification with their children as commendable or desirable. We have gained some perspective on one of life's most fundamental relationships to the extent that we understand our role as parents is to equip our children to lead happy, independent lives, to avoid imposing unnecessary barriers on their autonomy, and to allow them the freedom to choose their friends and form their own judgments as soon as possible. Furthermore, we recognize the importance of every adult, whether parent or child, having their own interests, as this prevents unhealthy interference in others' lives. Despite the shift from the old, often tyrannical dictatorship of parenthood motivated by deep affection to a more rational understanding of parental functions, there is no belief that the love between parents and children is diminishing in any way.

The comparison between a finished piece of work and a child is very apt: each must be nurtured and cared for as part of oneself during the early stages. However, with full maturity, there comes a time when each should have its independent identity. If we aim to maximize our potential in life, we must learn when to move on from one task to the next. Even the most productive among us could accomplish more if we learned to detach ourselves from completed tasks and redirect our energy towards future endeavors. Instead, we often linger and dwell on the outcomes of our recent engagements. To some extent, this is unavoidable; we need to understand the history and outcomes of our completed work in order to derive valuable lessons from them. However, here is where the average individual can learn from the exceptional. Abundance, as Edith Wharton noted, is the hallmark of true vocation, applicable to any field of endeavor. Genuine geniuses—whether a Leonardo, a Dickens, a Napoleon, or an Edison—are always moving forward. Versatility and abundance are not, as commonly believed, traits of mediocre craftsmen. When they manifest in a mediocre individual, they are, on the contrary, the very qualities they share with the great figures in their field.

We are so accustomed to completing a task and then pausing to observe its outcome that we often marvel at those who do not make the same mistake. Erroneously, we may believe that they must "push themselves" relentlessly to achieve what they manage to accomplish. However, this is not necessarily true. What has actually occurred is that the time, energy, and attention that lesser individuals invest in waiting for approval, listening to feedback, and pondering whether something could have been done better, is instead directed towards forging new paths. It's not that healthily prolific individuals are complacent or indifferent to genuine criticism; they understand that if anything relevant is said, they will hear it. Experience has taught them that we are never deaf to what truly matters to us. What they have learned is not to wait for feedback; as a result, their lives are twice as fulfilling and satisfying as those of us who struggle to discern when to release the results of our thoughts and labor—our intellectual offspring—to lead their own lives.

Imagination can help us comprehend how such sensible workers operate and suggest ways in which we can emulate them.

☆☆☆

On Codes and Standards

But what if you require approval and agreement at one stage of your work before proceeding to the next? What if your work contributes to a group effort? That, of course, is more complex, but imagination can still assist you. It can illustrate where you fit in the chain of causes that lead to a particular outcome, thus teaching you to be patient while your work is under consideration, to maintain equilibrium until a verdict is reached. Then, if the verdict is unfavorable—as it sometimes must be—you can choose one of two options: approach the same problem from a different angle, aiming to establish a solid working relationship with your collaborators this time, or present your reasons for believing in your original idea in a manner that demonstrates you're not defending it solely out of a sense of possessiveness.

The only way to accomplish this successfully is to establish a well-thought-out set of standards for each type of work you undertake, beforehand. If you wait until each task is completed, you might find yourself rationalizing after the fact, defending what's already done, and potentially overlooking genuine shortcomings.

Once again, we turn to imagination. If you were to envision the best possible example of the work you're about to undertake, what would it look like? Seek out the finest example of similar work available. What attributes does it possess? Which ones are absolutely essential? Which were introduced by the creator of that example? Armed with this analysis, draft a set of standards for your own use, prioritizing first those elements crucial for any chance of success; then those desirable if feasible to incorporate; and finally, but most crucial for your personal success, those elements that are your unique contribution.

Before diving into your task, set aside your own perspective and view your prospective task from the standpoint of your audience, the "ultimate consumer." Who stands to benefit from the endeavor? If you're a creative worker, who is your audience?

If you're selling a product, who is your target customer? If you were in their shoes, what would you want to see included in the offering? By imaginatively adopting the mindset of those through whom you hope to achieve success, you can often incorporate precisely those elements that will make your work irresistible.

Let's take a very familiar example to illustrate this point: kitchen equipment. For years, most stoves, sinks, and laundry tubs were made so low that the women using them quickly tired from the awkward positions they were forced into. Why did this persist? There was no good reason. But when someone, inspired by the thought of the comfort of those who would use these products, revolutionized kitchen equipment, things changed. Often, an improvement is right in front of us; a small, obvious change can transform an unsatisfactory product into one that offers greater convenience or usefulness. However, this change will only come from someone who is imaginative about their work, someone who can not only analyze the current form of an object but also empathize with the future user's experience.

Interestingly, it's often the creative worker who neglects to consider the desires of their audience when setting standards for their work. Yet, part of their goal must be to communicate an idea or emotion effectively to others. Failing to do so means failing in their intention. While constantly worrying about pleasing others can be detrimental to one's work, if recognition is part of your definition of success, understanding your audience becomes crucial. By knowing their tastes, you can not only meet their expectations but exceed them, delivering something they didn't even know they wanted.

After considering all these aspects and clarifying the direction your work should take, it's essential to evaluate it against a set of questions derived from well-defined standards before releasing it to the world. While the specifics may vary from one line of work to another and from person to person, the finished work should generally be assessed in the following manner:

Is what I have done as good as the best in its field?
Has it everything necessary for all ordinary purposes?
Have I added any special value through an original contribution?
Have I made it as attractive and convenient as possible for those who are its logical users? (Or audience, or clients.)
Have I considered whether there is another group to which it might also be made to appeal?
What more can I do before I release it from myself and send it out to make its own way? (Try reading these questions in two ways: as referring to an item of commerce; as an attitude towards a daily task.)
The artist will necessarily have a different set of questions, although they will be cognate with those above. As an example, one of our best poets asks herself these questions:
Have I conveyed what I thought?
Have I conveyed what I felt?
Is it as clear as I can make it?
Is it as distinguished or beautiful as its matter permits?

Again, if you are one of a group of workers, imagination can help you in still another way, by showing you where you stand in relation to those around you. When you have seen this, you can work out a code for yourself which will remove many of the irritations and dissatisfactions of your daily work. Have you ever been amused and enlightened by seeing a familiar room from the top of a stepladder; or, in mirrors set at angles to each other, seen yourself as objectively for a second or two as anyone else in the room? It is that effect you should try for in imagination. If you can see yourself and your fellow workers as impersonally as men on a chessboard, you can often find what it is that you are not doing, or what you are doing imperfectly, and move to correct the bad practice. Many of those who believe themselves overworked are doing less than they should ideally do and could do easily if they saw what is expected of them with imagination instead of anxiety. Often the excess work is something which they have almost officiously undertaken, many times from a real sense of duty and obligation. No large office is without one example of this type who is its reductio ad absurdum, the panicky job-grabber: from fear lest he, or, usually, she might possibly be considered as not doing all that is expected, or might be considered unnecessary to the organization, he gets a hundred small details in his hands, with the result that he is overworked, performance is not perfect, time is lost, and others who might be well occupied have time to idle and lose interest. If such a worker could see his position in perspective he could do more of the work he was really engaged for, do it better, and do it with less sense of strain and fatigue. Those executives and administrators who continually do far more than they can without incurring fatigue and irritability are frequently pandering to their own self-importance and conceit, although usually they would reject the charge with wrath. They are certainly allowing the Will to Fail to operate in their lives. It is good to extend one's normal activity till its capacity is reached—and that is far oftener much more than we habitually do rather than less—but the tasks taken on thereafter are the first steps towards failure—towards that trouble, beloved of Americans, the "nervous breakdown." When you have found your function, perform it very fully, but do not overstep it except in emergencies. In most large enterprises, or joint enterprises, there is—or should be—someone whose decisions are final. Sometimes each member of a partnership has the power of command or veto for one aspect of the work. Often these decisions are given after the opinions of all have been canvassed, or suggestions invited. Right here comes the necessity for a code: if the decision goes against you or your suggestion, abandon your own idea and cooperate in the decision wholeheartedly. If you feel that a truly grave mistake is being made, take a few hours to draw up the situation as you see it, show how you think the new decision will alter matters, why you think it is a mistake, or why an alternative plan should be adopted. Try to be as fair about this as you can. Often we think an alternative plan precious because, and only because, it is our own. "Pride of authorship" comes in.

Many of those who believe they have given up their own ideas and are working along other lines will unconsciously go on obstructing and objecting, holding up the work, trying to defeat its ends. The trouble here is that this obstructionism is often unconscious; but the way to escape the danger is to realize it as a possibility, and to look at yourself and your attitude scrupulously to be sure you are not putting up unnecessary hazards, doing your share of the new program slowly or indifferently—trying to bring about a failure, since your plan was ignored or modified.

If, on the other hand, you are the one whose decisions must be accepted, you will save yourself trouble later by watching the initial stages of the work to be sure that some such unconscious sabotage is not going on. A quick challenge to the troublesome person whose feelings have been hurt will sometimes whip a whole program into shape which might otherwise fail. And by such watching you can see that each is doing the work assigned to him.

A little imaginative overseeing of a staff or partnership in the early stages of any activity will often result in clearing up a disorder of long standing.

Perhaps, however, you are really miscast, and your usefulness would be on, say, the planning end of an enterprise rather than the executive, where you are placed. In that case, your problem is to bring your talents to the attention of your superior officers with as little crowding and bustling as possible. Learn to write clear, short, definite memoranda and present them to your immediate superior until you are perfectly certain that he will never act upon them. In no other circumstances are you justified in going over his head. Try also to be willing to see your work and suggestions acted upon without receiving immediate acknowledgment that the ideas originated with you. This frequently happens in a large organization, and to sulk or stand out for having your rights recognized in every case will only cancel the advance you might have been able to make. If your good idea is one of a series and not a flash in the pan, you can be sure your caliber will eventually make itself felt. If not, the organization is a bad one for you, and you should set about finding a better connection as soon as possible.

Partnerships, especially the universal partnership of husband and wife, are typically unique situations. Generally, the guideline should be to avoid assuming the normal role of the other partner unless there is almost undeniable evidence that failing to do so will disrupt a vital balance. Often, fulfilling one's own responsibilities competently is sufficient to prompt complementary actions from the other partner. In any partnership, once you're confident in fulfilling your own duties, if there are still apparent weaknesses, they can usually be discussed, reasons understood, and corrections made. Occasionally, this may not be possible. Only those in such a relationship know when it's impossible to discuss matters due to the partner's oversensitivity or blindness. In such cases, take on as much of the overlooked responsibility as you can handle well, but not more. There's always the chance of sudden insight or delayed growth, jeopardized if you shoulder too much. However, be mindful that when you must take on tasks not your own, willingly accept these responsibilities; ensure they're not forced upon you. Undertaking tasks with awareness will seldom lead to later feelings of martyrdom or resentment.

Once you've envisioned your role both as an individual and as part of a group, society, or partnership, you're prepared to educate, discipline, and train yourself until you achieve maximum effectiveness.

☆☆☆

Twelve Disciplines

I

There are many small ways in which we can sharpen and expand our minds—two qualities crucial for those aiming to live successfully. Often, we easily fall into the trap of settling into a routine that allows us to complete our daily tasks with minimal effort and conscious thought. This wouldn't be a problem if we used the time saved by our routines wisely. However, the reality is quite different. We tend to apply this tendency for routine to all aspects of our lives, becoming mentally and spiritually weaker, less adventurous, and less willing to try new things with each passing day, relying on the rigidity of habit.

Our habits manage most of our daily activities; we navigate through our work using only the part of our intellect that has been trained to handle the specific problems at hand. When faced with a new idea or situation, we resort to analogy and act based on the prejudices or emotions it stirs within us. Even those who embark on self-improvement endeavors often exercise only a specific mental skill set, accumulating knowledge about various subjects such as the religions of India, the works of Charles Dickens, or the birds of Southern California, and considering themselves "improved" by doing so.

While fact-gathering is an intellectual activity and can be valuable when accompanied or preceded by training in independent judgment, it alone does not fully engage the mind or equip one to utilize all its capabilities effectively.

Even those who consider themselves hard workers often lack the mental training necessary to truly optimize their lives. One significant reason for this, as repeatedly emphasized by Dr. Alexis Carrel in his book "Man, the Unknown," is that the benefits of civilization come with drawbacks. We are no longer required to endure extreme temperatures or cycles of abundance and scarcity; artificial lighting makes night as bright as day, and entertainment from newspapers and radio keeps us distracted. Dr. Carrel notes that "the exercise of the adaptive functions appears to be indispensable to the optimum development of man." However, we have allowed ourselves to become soft, relinquishing our ingenuity and avoiding responsibility whenever possible, until we develop a fear and aversion to the very idea of "discipline."

Yet, discipline entails restraint to cultivate the qualities essential for a fulfilling life. Mental discipline should be akin to the rigorous training an athlete undergoes to refine their body. We must first assess our minds, then work on strengthening them, making them more adaptable, stretching their limits, refining their precision—in essence, putting them through rigorous training to extract maximum utility and benefit from them.

To achieve this, we must learn to impose strict standards on ourselves—a challenging task for a generation softened by modern conveniences and indulged in constant self-analysis. Some of us fear and resist discipline, even when self-imposed for a noble purpose, living our lives torn between habit and impulse under the illusion that only through such a stance can we attain true freedom. However, as Aristotle stated, "Freedom is obedience to self-imposed rules," a notion as relevant today as it was two millennia ago.

We need to reintroduce strength and agility into our lives, enabling us to seamlessly transition from one task to another, adjusting our approach, intensity, and effort just like a skilled tennis player adapts to the changing tactics of a formidable opponent. If we could predict the exact challenges we'll face each day, we could prepare accordingly, and flexibility and ingenuity would be unnecessary. However, since life doesn't work that way, we must train ourselves to confront the myriad demands placed upon us, instead of simply excelling in a few areas that come naturally to us while clumsily navigating through others.

The disciplines recommended here are drawn from diverse cultures around the globe. Those familiar with philosophy and religion will encounter practices advocated by wise figures from various countries: from India and Spain to Greece and China—and even from traditional finishing schools. Some practices are universal to any culture that values mental or spiritual development, such as observing periods of silence. None of these disciplines are arbitrary in the sense of being pointless; each serves to develop or fortify a mental faculty crucial for leading a purposeful life under one's own guidance.

Not all of these disciplines will be equally beneficial to everyone; however, before dismissing any of them, examine yourself to determine if you're rejecting it simply because it requires a bit more self-restraint than you find enjoyable. Many of these practices will pose challenges at some point, akin to the stiffness and soreness experienced when using a new muscle during athletic training. Just as you can only strengthen a muscle by subjecting it to resistance, you must experience some level of discomfort to ensure that your efforts are effective. Therefore, while engaging in these mental exercises, if you don't feel any discomfort from fully embracing each one, if there's no resistance stemming from breaking old habits and adopting new ways of action, it's possible that the discipline in question isn't what you truly need. In that case, replace it with another discipline that requires endurance and effort.

II. THE TWELVE DISCIPLINES

1.

The initial exercise entails spending an hour daily without uttering a word except in response to direct inquiries. This should occur within your usual social circle, without giving the impression that you're sulking or suffering from a headache. Maintain a regular demeanor; simply refrain from speaking. Respond to questions succinctly, providing a thorough and adequate answer but avoiding additional comments suggested by the question or answer. Don't attempt to prompt further questions from your conversation partner. Surprisingly, this proves challenging even for those naturally reserved. We're so accustomed to speaking whenever we meet others, merely to demonstrate friendliness and accessibility, that we chatter incessantly whenever the opportunity arises.

This practice is prevalent in many cultures with ancient religions and yields various outcomes of significant value. The reactions to this exercise vary greatly depending on individual temperaments. One common observation is that we seldom articulate precisely what we mean on the first try. We hastily speak, realize from the other person's expression that we haven't conveyed our message clearly or have misspoken, and then attempt to clarify. However, this process may not achieve the desired understanding, leading to further attempts. Meanwhile, the previous unsuccessful attempts remain in the listeners' minds, muddling the communication.

One participant reported feeling initially as if they weren't present at all. Then, there was a phase where their silence seemed to fill the entire room, providing an impersonal perspective of the surroundings. While speaking, they naturally occupied the center of attention, but in silence, the group dynamic shifted. At the end of the hour, they perceived themselves alternating between being central to the conversation, on the periphery, or entirely detached from the interests of those around them.

Another participant noted that as their silence became noticeable, their friends' reactions were quite revealing. Two friends, not fully aware of what made the situation unusual, exhibited discomfort. One became overly ingratiating, another grew confrontational and eventually accused the silent individual of feeling superior, just as the hour concluded and speech resumed. A third friend, typically quiet in the group, became excessively talkative, seemingly trying to restore a perceived imbalance, only returning to silence when the observer resumed speaking naturally.

A woman shared, with much amusement, that she had never experienced such personal success as during the hour she spent silently smiling at a party. Her silence seemed to attract attention and pose a challenge in a way her previous cheerfulness had never achieved.

However, all participants agreed on one point: during the silence, they felt a sense of empowerment growing within them. When they resumed speaking, it was with a deliberate and purposeful manner, always aware that the option of silence was available whenever needed. One participant concluded her reflection with a quote from Meredith, which she claimed she had never fully comprehended until then: "It is the silence of the god we fear, not his wrath; Silence is the unbearable repartee."

2.

Learn to devote half an hour each day exclusively to thinking about one subject. As simple as it sounds, it is initially quite challenging. Beginners should start by focusing on their chosen subject for just five minutes a day, gradually increasing the duration until reaching half an hour. Begin with a tangible object: a flower, a bottle of ink, a scarf. Instead of having it physically present, construct it in your mind. For example, with a flower, describe it using each of your senses. Then, consider its growth, location, symbolism, and uses. From this basic starting point, progress to contemplating a specific problem, and eventually, to an abstract concept. Initially, select subjects that genuinely interest you. Once you've trained your mind to stay focused without wavering, start choosing subjects randomly by pointing your finger at a newspaper or book page and contemplating the first idea suggested by the lines you touch.

You may find it helpful to begin this exercise with a pencil and pad, making a mark on the paper whenever you notice your attention drifting. If you're quick to recognize when your mind starts to wander, you'll likely fill the paper quite a bit during the initial days. Fortunately, improvement in this area comes fairly quickly. Within a week for some, or a month for others, you may find your pad nearly blank by the end of your half-hour session. The value of this exercise should be evident to anyone aspiring to engage in original work or introduce new procedures of any kind. Initially, it's best to practice this exercise alone, but eventually, you should be able to do it even amidst distractions, such as during your commute to and from work.

(Note that the recommendation here is not to hold your mind fixed on one object, as in certain Indian disciplines or the Christian practice called "recollection." Instead, you are to focus on one subject only; nothing more. The other practice induces a slightly hypnotic state and is not suitable for our purposes here.)

This practice essentially embodies the concepts of "application" and "concentration" taught to us all during our school days. It's quite enlightening to realize how imperfectly we learned that lesson then, or at any subsequent time! However, once mastered, it proves immensely beneficial. Anyone capable of it can quickly pick up a foreign language. While the accent may not be perfect, reading books and newspapers becomes easy, and a functional vocabulary for navigating the foreign land can be acquired in less than a month.

Furthermore, in any competitive endeavor, those who have trained themselves to think steadily, without distraction, will reach conclusions more quickly. But the advantages of this practice are too obvious to require further emphasis.

3.

Compose a letter without using the words: I, me, my, mine. Ensure the letter flows smoothly and remains engaging. If the recipient detects anything unusual about it, the exercise has failed. This practice, along with others of its kind, offers us a chance to gain perspective on ourselves. To write a compelling letter of this nature, one must redirect their focus outward, temporarily setting aside preoccupations and self-centered concerns. As a result, we return to our own lives feeling rejuvenated.

4.

Speak for fifteen minutes daily without employing the words: I, me, my, mine.

5.

Write a letter adopting a "successful" or tranquil tone. Avoid any falsehoods or misrepresentations. Instead, focus on aspects or activities that can be honestly portrayed in such a manner, indicating through the letter's tone that, at the time of writing, you are not feeling discouraged in any way. This exercise serves a dual purpose. Firstly, it offers a simple method to shift from a negative and disheartened mindset to a positive and healthy one. Despite initially seeming challenging to find enough positive content for the letter, one soon realizes that several aspects of life are progressing smoothly and satisfactorily, albeit overlooked while dwelling on disappointment and frustration. Secondly, sending such letters to nearly every correspondent helps overcome a significant obstacle to effectively managing one's affairs.

Letter-writing is often relegated to spare moments in our day. When feeling listless, bored, tired, or disheartened, we pick up our pen and write to our loved ones. Unfortunately, we tend to send melancholy, gloomy notes, and subsequently receive consolatory or sympathetic responses. Although sometimes these replies arrive when we're feeling fairly well or even jubilant, it takes considerable strength of character to resist indulging in self-pity. Presented with the option of either slipping back into a martyr-like mood or feeling rather foolish, many choose the former. Thus, we perpetuate a cycle of self-pity and despondency, sharing the latest bad news when we correspond again. A complete break from self-pity and despair is essential for achieving success.

6.

This exercise is a direct practice from all the finishing schools for young ladies that have ever existed: pause on the threshold of any crowded room you are about to enter, and take a moment to consider your relation to those inside. Many a reserved and tranquil woman can attribute her ability to handle challenging situations competently to this simple aspect of her school training. For years (and perhaps still today), it was customary to instruct young girls to pause briefly at the door of the room they were entering until they located their hostess, and then the guest of honor. If there was no designated guest of honor, they were instructed to approach the oldest person in the room. Once identified, they would enter the room and promptly go to their hostess for a welcome and to "make their manners." Following this, they would seek an opportunity to converse briefly with the guest of honor. Only after fulfilling these obligations were they free to pursue their own plans or interests. A girl who thoroughly grasped this lesson learned something invaluable: the ability to assess a room full of people at a glance, discerning first their obligations and then their potential companionship or personal interests.

There is a somewhat absurd notion prevailing today that engaging in such deliberate forethought about any social occasion is hypocritical or snobbish, and that there is virtue in impulsively diving into any situation, seizing whatever presents itself without much thought, and disregarding the rest. Taking a moment to anticipate the various possibilities and relationships in the upcoming occasion doesn't make one "artificial." Instead, it prevents one from being rushed into activities that are incongruous, getting stuck in conversations unrelated to genuine interests, or missing opportunities to engage with real friends or individuals whose conversation holds value. Even with the most conscientious planning, there remains enough room for the unforeseen and unexpected to preserve spontaneity. Nonetheless, the goal is to exert as much voluntary control over our lives as possible. Sometimes, despite our best intentions, we may not achieve what we hoped for in that moment of anticipation. However, if we have taken the effort to consider all possibilities beforehand, we can easily shift our focus to a secondary interest, without missing out on every opportunity simply because one didn't pan out.

7.

Once you have mastered or reacquired the previous exercise, proceed to an old piece of advice from seventeenth-century France: keep a new acquaintance talking about themselves without allowing them to realize what you're doing. Initially, deflect any polite reciprocal questions in a manner that doesn't make your listener feel brushed off. As you genuinely become interested in your companion, you'll find yourself increasingly engaged, particularly if you possess kindness or imagination. Gradually, any lingering self-consciousness will dissipate. Even if your companion doesn't inquire about you, it doesn't matter; at the very least, you'll have gained insight into how the world appears to someone else, broadening your perspective. However, if you do eventually discuss yourself in response to later questions, you'll know precisely how much to share, what common interests you have, and whether pursuing a friendship with that person would be desirable.

(It may be necessary to state plainly that acting consciously doesn't equate to acting coldly. Exerting control over one's actions doesn't diminish genuine humanity; rather, it enhances it. Engaging in an outward effort voluntarily, instead of being entirely absorbed in ourselves and oblivious to the moods or interests of others except as they relate to us, allows us to break free from our constricting self-centeredness through a more pleasant route. The other party in this interaction is not a victim of calculated manipulation; instead, they are reassured that they aren't subjected to our blind selfishness.)

8.

The exact opposite of the above exercises, and infinitely harder to do with intention: Talk exclusively about yourself and your interests without complaining, boasting, or (if possible) boring your companion. Make yourself and your activities as interesting as you can to the person you're speaking to.

This is an excellent discipline for those who tend to talk excessively about themselves. This exaggeration of their weakness confronts them with the ordeal they impose on their friends every time. When consciously engaging in concentrated discussion about one's own interests, every sign of indifference, boredom, restlessness, or impatience, every desire to switch topics that might escape notice while one is self-absorbed, becomes painfully obvious. Both the exercise and the weakness are usually abandoned gratefully after one or two attempts.

However, there are other benefits to be gained from this exercise. It becomes apparent that discussing trivial, mundane, or repetitive aspects of one's life can lead to boredom in our listeners. Conversely, if we have genuinely interesting experiences, have approached a situation with more imagination than usual, or are embarking on something new, we are more likely to captivate our audience. The realization that we might benefit from broadening our interests, undertaking new adventures, or injecting more imagination into our everyday lives is hard to escape in such cases. We quickly learn to avoid discussing our latest illness, our children's latest antics, our pets' remarkable intelligence, or today's stroke of bad luck as opening topics in adult conversation. If you find yourself with someone who persists in such mundane conversations, consciously introduce a deeper or more engaging topic when it's your turn to speak. If you find that they stubbornly resist such attempts at elevating the conversation, you may need to make a decision.

Sometimes, despite any limitations, there is such warmth, sweetness, and genuine feeling in even a limited friend that one cannot imagine abandoning the relationship. However, at times, we discover to our dismay that we've formed a connection with someone solely because we can chatter on about the trivialities of our lives in their presence, without any deeper bond. In such cases, it's a plain obligation to withdraw from the association as soon as possible without causing harm to the other person, to refuse to waste your own energy and time, or to be complicit in wasting theirs. If you've been guilty (as many of us have) of forming such a weak association, the first step towards correction should be to see if it can be transformed into a genuine friendship that is stimulating and strengthening. Only when all hope of that is lost should the relationship be ended.

9.

The correction of the "I-mean," the "As-a-matter-of-fact" habit, requires cooperation. If you realize that you have developed a verbal mannerism, seek assistance from the friend with whom you communicate most fluently and emotionally. It's relatively easy to control such a mannerism in the company of someone we barely know, but during intense conversation, the offending phrase will slip into nearly every other sentence. Explain to your friend that you're overusing phrases like "and so on" to the point of absurdity. Ask them to observe and signal whenever they hear you use it, without interrupting the conversation. The ensuing dialogue may become disjointed, with more laughter than discussion for a while, but you'll start to gain control over the habit. After two or three sessions, the phrase will be completely eradicated—except when you intentionally choose to use it.

10.

Plan two hours of a day and adhere to the plan. If you're working independently as a freelancer, any day will suffice. If not, choose a Sunday or holiday for experimentation. Design the schedule partly based on your usual routine, partly different from it. For example: 7:30–8 Breakfast and newspaper 8–8:20 Mail 8:20–9:25 Organize books by subject matter 9:25–9:30 Make a phone call (if it's a weekday) for an appointment you've been postponing. If it's Sunday or a holiday, go for a walk. The complexity or variety of tasks has little bearing on this practice. The key is to transition from one activity to the next precisely at the designated moment, not approximately. If you're only halfway through the newspaper, it's regrettable. However, you must set it aside and attend to your mail—previously neglected. If it's a day without incoming mail, utilize the twenty minutes for letter-writing. If you have spare time, send a couple of cards or jot down notes for another letter on another day. Regardless of your progress with correspondence by 8:20, shift your focus to arranging books. At least one planned activity should hold a reasonable level of interest for you. If it's not organizing books, then clipping articles from a magazine can serve as a replacement, or even thoroughly tidying a room. This discipline serves two purposes: firstly, to reacquaint ourselves with following orders, and secondly, to illustrate how poorly we estimate the time needed for any given task. Many printers have likely grumbled about editors or make-up men who try to cram too many letters on a line, lamenting, "He must think we've got rubber type." Similarly, most of us assume our days have rubber hours. Even suburbanites, who know from experience that it takes precisely seventeen minutes to walk from the shower to the train station, casually plan to squeeze half a day's work into a couple of hours after lunch. We expect time to be infinitely accommodating, refusing to acknowledge its limitations. Yet, it's feasible to learn—by initially planning two hours of a day, then three, then four, and so forth until we've mapped out and lived an effective eight-hour day (at minimum)—how to utilize time optimally. While rigid scheduling for an entire day isn't always feasible or desirable, periodically living by a timetable will rejuvenate our appreciation for the value of time and teach us what we can reasonably expect of ourselves when we don't squander it. For those who need a stern reminder: psychiatrist Dr. Paul Bousfeld argues that the hallmark of the incurable egotist is their failure to account for the actual time required for any given activity. Firmly, though unconsciously, believing that the world revolves around them, and certain of their magical ability to halt the progress of the sun and the moon, they go through life astonished at Time's resistance to meeting them halfway. They're consistently tardy to appointments, behind on obligations, perpetually assuming more work or accepting more invitations than they can manage if they were twins. They either learn from their mistakes or meet an unfortunate fate.

11.

This is the most challenging of all. It will seem so arbitrary to many readers that they will not even try to apply it. It is arbitrary; that is its very essence. It is less necessary for those living in the midst of large families than for persons living alone, or those who are alone most of the time. Remembering the quotation given above from Dr. Carrel, arrange to put yourself into situations where you must act non-habitually, where you must adapt yourself. Members of the Army, the Navy, the priesthood, some societies, are constantly in a state of living under orders; and we recognize in them a resiliency that is absent from the characters of most men and women who live according to their own convenience. It is not easy to get this resiliency back into our lives, but it is a quality too valuable to be lost. If the following recommendation seems somewhat too dramatic, almost too ridiculous, be assured that the results will show the worth of the discipline. On a number of slips of paper—twelve will do to start with—write instructions like these: "Go twenty miles from home, using ordinary conveyance." (In other words, don't just get out a car or hire a taxi, if you can afford it, and drive somewhere. Take street-cars, buses, ferries, subways.) "Go twelve hours without food." "Go eat a meal in the unlikeliest place you can find." A restaurant in a totally foreign quarter of a city is good here. Asking for food at a farm-house is better, if you are hardy enough to be so unconventional. "Say nothing all day except in answer to questions." "Stay up all night and work." And this, by the way, is the most valuable order of them all. You must plan to work steadily and quietly, resisting every temptation to lie down for a few moments, but relaxing very slightly against the chair-back every hour or so, bracing yourself to your work again the moment lassitude threatens to overcome you. Only those who have actually done this realize that there are depths to our minds which we seldom plumb, accustomed as we are to succumb to the first attack of fatigue, or staying awake only so long as we have outer stimulation. Seal these slips of paper in twelve envelopes, shuffle them thoroughly and put them in a drawer. Whenever you think of it, shuffle them again. Every other week, or on a given day of each month, pick one of the envelopes, open it, and perform your own command. It may be raining pitchforks on the day you command yourself to travel twenty miles by common carrier; nevertheless, unless your state of health absolutely forbids it, you go. If you are doing an intensive piece of work, one monthly exercise of this sort is enough. If not, the oftener you can be arbitrary with yourself—without turning into a restless jumping-jack, it goes without saying—the better for your character eventually. There need not be twelve different orders on your slips. If you can think of activities which are genuinely difficult for you to do, which go against the grain but which you yet know would be valuable training for you, include them. One young man of my acquaintance who was abnormally shy insisted to himself that he should get into conversation with at least three strangers daily. Any activity you choose should be both corrective and unusual, cutting abruptly across your usual routine.

12.

An alternative method is this: from time to time, give yourself a day on which you say "Yes" to every request made of you which is at all reasonable. The more you tend to withdraw from society in your leisure time, the more valuable this will be. You may find yourself invited to go sleigh-riding in your twenty-four hours; you may be invited to change your job. The sleigh-ride should certainly be accepted, however much you may dislike straw, thick blankets, and cold weather. The job-changing, fortunately, can be subjected to examination since it is only "reasonable" activities that you are to undertake without second thought. Don't be afraid that nothing will occur on that day; it is astonishing how many small requests we can turn aside daily rather than interrupt our even course. The consequences may be far-reaching, often educational, sometimes extremely advantageous. Nevertheless, do not jump to the conclusion that because one day of this sort has brought so many interesting possibilities to light, every day should be led in that manner. On the contrary; denying oneself an opportunity now and then is just as enlightening, particularly for those who waste too much time in party-going, theatres, and so on. Such individuals should plan to decline many invitations and spend the time in intensive self-cultivation.

On this system, work out other disciplines that are good for your individual case. There are two ways of making them. First, become aware of some weakness or inadequate performance on your part; then decide, perhaps after experimentation, whether the way to correct it is to set yourself to do the exact opposite or whether—as in curing the habit of talking too much about one's own interests—acting in a ludicrous and over-emphasized parody of the failing will be more effective.

Once you grasp the idea, you will find these disciplines not only helpful but genuinely amusing. In many cases, they replace the rather haphazard puzzle-solving activities which call on somewhat the same capacities. By matching your wits against yourself, you take on the shrewdest and wiliest antagonist you can have, and consequently, a victorious outcome in this duel of wits brings a great feeling of triumph. Finally, when one is in training, one can call at will on any of the mental traits which have been strengthened or exercised in these ways and find that it performs exactly and quickly.

But, as you begin to take pleasure in these exercises, remind yourself that they are means, not ends. In gaining control of your mind, you are not yet using it officially, so to speak. You are still in your probationary period. Have you ever met one of those health-seekers who eat just so many ounces of food per day, walk just so many miles, or play just so many games of handball, sit in the sun or under a sunlamp just so many minutes—and then lead the dullest of personal lives? They have made themselves into magnificently healthy creatures—for no purpose whatsoever. You are training your mind in order to engage it in definite activity, so do not put off too long the matter of getting at your original plans.

III

Still considering what aids we can find to successful living, but now in the way of direct support for ourselves, there are various ways in which we can make the process smoother. One of the best is to follow the suggestion of Franklin, in his Autobiography, and to check daily on our progress by means of a small, specially prepared notebook. Franklin himself drew up a list of thirteen Virtues, and under each wrote a maxim embodying the sense of that virtue to his mind. For instance, under Temperance, he wrote "Eat not to dullness; drink not to elevation"; under Silence: "Speak not but what may benefit others or yourself; avoid trifling conversation"; and so went on, through Order, Resolution, Frugality, and the rest. It is hardly possible to draw up a better set, but—and perhaps it is one more sign of the softening of the race—for most purposes, the six matters which we find most troublesome will seem quite enough for our present purposes. Each will have his own set of faults to be corrected. But let us say, for instance, that you decide you could do more work if you would; that you are shy; that you take too long to make up your mind; that you talk too much (and timidity and talkativeness are by no means mutually exclusive vices); that you eat at odd hours or the wrong things; that you sleep too long (or not enough). Your notebook-page should look like this:

	S	M	T	W	T	F	S
WORK	√						
COURAGE							
DECISION	√ √						
SPEECH	√ √						
MEALS	√						
SLEEP							

The checks represent your estimate of the number of times you successfully resisted the temptation to act in the unsatisfactory way. As you find yourself able to fill any of the squares of your notebook each day—in other words, when you have eradicated the trouble-making fault—you can retire that classification and replace it with another which you may have noticed. If you soon outgrow the need of the notebook, splendid. It can be kept in a convenient drawer, though, as a reminder. Then there is the matter of getting into the day. Those who wake fully each morning would find it hard to believe how many of their fellows suffer from not being fully in command of their faculties in the morning. If you belong to the latter crew, don't hesitate to imitate the Katherine Mansfield hero who woke, opened his eyes, and saw the sign he had put up for himself: "Get out of bed at once." What is more, if you know—as so many of us do—that at midnight you have a genuine inspiration which your morning's prosaic mood leads you to disregard, write yourself a note about it. Be pretty firm about the matter; put it sharply. Say to yourself, in writing, "You're an idiot if you don't at least see whether Macy's would like that idea. Make an appointment today!" Often nothing more is needed to make the prosy, unimaginative daylight mood break up and allow the intenser one to return. One of the most famous men in America constantly sends himself post-cards, and occasionally notes. He explained the card-sending as being his way of relieving his memory of unnecessary details. In his pocket, he carries a few postals addressed to his office. I was with him one threatening day when he looked out the restaurant window, drew a card from his pocket and wrote on it. Then he threw it across the table to me with a grin. It was addressed to himself at his office, and said "Put your rain-coat with your hat." At the office, he had other cards addressed to himself at home. Rewarding oneself for successful work—even in addition to the success—is another way of promoting proper action. If you get yourself some small luxury when, and only when, your notebook shows a week of satisfactory marks, you may go to slightly more trouble to turn away from your faults. Get into the habit of being both strict and friendly toward yourself: demand a certain standard of performance; approve of yourself, even reward yourself, if you attain it. Far too often we pursue just the wrong tactics. When we should be acting we indulge or excuse ourselves for inactivity; we then upbraid and punish ourselves ruthlessly and futilely. The scolding is futile because we somehow feel that if we have been severe and cutting to ourselves, we have in some way atoned for the fault of non-performance. We have not, of course. We have not done what we planned, and we have discouraged and hurt ourselves into the bargain.

☆☆☆

—And the Best of Luck!

Summing up, then, we have as the first tenet of success: Act as if it were impossible to fail. Beginning to put this into practice, we discover that the first demand upon us is that we should reclaim as much as possible of the energy which now goes into revery or into time-killing, and devote it to purposeful activity, to action-toward-an-end. We act by ignoring all memories or apprehensions of failure, by refusing to attach importance to temporary discomfort or past pain. We learn not to court frustration by using an attitude or tone which leaves any opportunity for rebuff or noncooperation. We exercise our minds in trial-performances in order to have them fully under our control when the occasion to use them in an expert way arises. With the imagination, we painlessly explore all the possible reaches of our lives and constantly provide ourselves with prospects of future interests to such an extent that we shall not fall back into daydreaming. We deliberately make for ourselves an invigorating mental climate, and in this atmosphere, freed of doubts and anxieties, we act. In the last few chapters, we have been considering these facets of successful action one by one. Now it must be remembered that, however correct and suggestive such detailed considerations may be, they suffer badly in one manner: their tempo, so to speak, has had to be altered in order to show them minutely. A slow-motion picture of ball-players in action, of golfers, of a tennis-match, is sometimes of inestimable value to those who are learning to play. The muscular effort behind a sudden dexterous turn of the body, in its normal tempo far too quick for the eye to catch, is shown in the retarded film in all its subtlety. But we gain our insight into the technique of difficult plays by losing sight, for the moment, of another aspect. You will remember how, in such pictures, the player glides languorously through the air, the ball curves slowly towards the racquet, touches it with a soft impact and slides slowly away again. Illuminating as these pictures are, they are also always irresistibly comic: the leap, the crack, the rapidity of the game as we know it is gone, replaced by a twilit, dreaming gentleness. Now, to consider the technique of success in these pages, we have had to sacrifice pace to analysis in just this way. The actual tempo of success, while it should not have the nervousness or strain that is almost inevitable in a competitive contest, is quicker, smoother, more brisk than any book analyzing it can ever show. There is a delightful conciseness in successful action. "I know I'm doing a good picture if I'm painting just as fast as I can move," a great artist said to a group of friends recently. "The minute I dabble I know I'm stalling, that there's something I'm not seeing right; when I'm right it's almost like play."

There is undoubtedly something game-like about pertinent activity: those distressful clichés of a few years ago, "the advertising game," "the engineering game," "the restaurant game," had some excuse in reality. The vocabulary of men who are successful in the sense that they have amassed huge fortunes abounds in terms taken over from the jargon of sports: "A fast one," "Out of bounds," and so on. And however unlike the big-business ambition of such a man one's own personal idea of success may be, there is something to be deduced from the frequency of recreation-terms when stories of success are in question. Purposeful action seems quicker, clearer, more straightforward and enjoyable than any other. In reality, you may be working more slowly and carefully than ordinarily; still, the fact that there is no confusion of issues, no part of your mind off wool-gathering as you move, gives an unmistakable "tone" to activities which are being carried on in the proper way.

It is just this tone that you are setting yourself to recapture by imagination when you remember the mood of an earlier success. Once you have found it in the past, made use of it for present action, and noted the similarity in pace which results, you will soon be able to strike the right rhythm without the elaborate preliminary imaginative activity. Further, this rhythm sometimes crops out unexpectedly, in the middle of unimportant events; it is a promise that, if you can get away and at work, you will find yourself "in vein." So you will come to recognize its onset and be able to turn it to your advantage. This feeling of pace, or tone, or rhythm—it represents itself differently to differing temperaments—will be your evidence that you are headed the right way. This is no recommendation to hasten your physical action in working. That may or may not come to pass. Very often it does; in other cases undue haste has been one of the contributions of the Will to Fail, which, aping the decisiveness of authoritative motion, allowed several essentials to good work to be overlooked or skimped. It is not so much any real briskness that is being considered here as it is the fact that unimpeded movement in a forward direction is pleasant and rhythmical, movement which goes unwaveringly towards success.

Let us, for another reductio ad absurdum, consider one great class of successes, of which almost everyone has had some personal experience, or at the very least has met in the lives of those about him: the state called the courage of desperation. In the most extreme cases, this courage arises because some catastrophe or series of misfortunes has completely wiped out every alternative to success. "He has nothing to lose," we say of one in this situation. Very well, then; he acts with a directness and daring which he could not ordinarily command. So often that it has become a matter of legend for us, this action is attended with overwhelming success. If you will remember the third victim of the Will to Fail in an earlier chapter, you will recall that he had made a state of desperation into a superstitious prerequisite to accomplishment. Quite misreading the situation, he came to believe that the prospect of utter vanquishment would, each time, cause Fate to relent. What he entirely overlooked was that when he had reached such straits that he dared not fail he invariably acted as he should always act: as if it were impossible to fail. Without exception in this state he succeeded. Inextricably involved in the meshes of his bad and emotional thinking, he invited failure as the only way to spur himself to effort. To his acquaintances he inevitably recalled the crazy hero of world-wide fame, the man who hit himself on the head with a hammer because it felt so good when he stopped. It was and is all very serious to him. But remove the absurdity from these examples of the courage of desperation, and we have the sense. Desperation does cut off one alternative. But desperation is not needed, is not the only tool which will cut away the possibility of failure. Imagination will do the work even better and more neatly. And we are left with Courage-facing-in-the-right-direction. Courage facing in the right direction is the sine qua non of success. It is to reach that stage that we put ourselves through exercises in flexibility and restraint, learn to turn imagination away from apprehension and into useful channels, determine to act wisely in minor matters in order to store up courage for the major issues of our lives. We use our heads to get the greatest good from our gifts and abilities, refusing ourselves the weakening privileges of dreaming, avoiding responsibilities, following the line of least resistance, acting childishly. Success, for any sane adult, is exactly equivalent to doing his best. What that best may be, what its farthest reaches may include, we can discover only by freeing ourselves completely from the Will to Fail.

☆*The End*☆